Human Resource Transformation

Human Resource Transformation

Demonstrating Strategic Leadership in the Face of Future Trends

WILLIAM J. ROTHWELL, PhD, SPHR

ROBERT K. PRESCOTT, PhD, SPHR

MARIA W. TAYLOR

Davies-Black Publishing
Mountain View, California

Published by Davies-Black Publishing, a division of CPP, Inc., 1055 Joaquin Road, 2nd Floor, Mountain View, CA 94043; 800-624-1765.

Special discounts on bulk quantities of Davies-Black books are available to corporations, professional associations, and other organizations. For details, contact the Director of Marketing and Sales at Davies-Black Publishing: 650–691–9123; fax 650–623–9271.

Visit the Davies-Black Publishing Web site at www.daviesblack.com.

12 11 10 09 08 10 9 8 7 6 5 4 3 2 1
Printed in the United States of America.

Library of Congress Cataloging-in-Publication Data

Rothwell, William J.
   Human resource transformation : demonstrating strategic leadership
   in the face of future trends / William J. Rothwell, Robert K. Prescott,
   Maria W. Taylor.—1st ed.
      p. cm.
   Includes bibliographical references and index.
   ISBN 978-0-89106-251-6 (hardcover)
   1. Personnel management. 2. Manpower planning. 3. Organizational change.
   I. Prescott, Robert K. II. Taylor, Maria W. III. Title.
   HF5549.R6358 2008
   658.3'01—dc22

                         2007037234

FIRST EDITION
First printing 2008

To my wife, Marcelina; daughter, Candice; son, Froilan; and grand-son, Aden. **William J. Rothwell**

For the late Sanford B. Morton Jr., who taught me the foundations of human resource management, and beyond this inspired in me the focus to constantly redefine the requirements for HR in fostering organizational success. **Robert K. Prescott**

To my two wonderful sons, Brendan and David. **Maria W. Taylor**

Contents

....

Part Three
ENACTING A NEW ROLE OF HR LEADERSHIP

Figures, Tables, Worksheets, and Transformation in Action Examples

....

Tables

Worksheets

Transformation in Action Examples

Preface

··

This book was conceived in 2004. At that time, one of the book's authors, William Rothwell, was called in to a large Chinese industrial plant and asked by the vice president of human resources (HR) of that organization to help the plant meet the surprising requirement of corporate headquarters to slash 40 percent of the plant's HR staff in less than one month. When the stunned vice president of HR asked corporate headquarters how the department could continue to do what it had always done with a greatly reduced staff, the corporate leaders agreed that that would be impossible. The department would have to "recharter itself," coming up with a new mission, goals, and objectives to support business efforts. From that experience—and, since then, others like it—Rothwell has become acutely aware of how often HR transformation is occurring in major companies. But often these efforts are not well conceived, and leaders are unaware of the many possible strategic decisions for HR and the organization that they could make. This book, then, is intended to provide practical advice, ideas, and suggestions for how to advance HR transformation efforts.

Is HR Dead?

"HR Is Dead, Long Live HR," writes Shari Caudron (2005, p. 3). "In this era of human capital, HR is experiencing seismic change. Outsourcing is swiftly taking over. If HR stands still, it's doomed. But if it changes, its business clout can be more potent than ever." Caudron continues to depict the two sides of this dramatic change by stating that "the field is in the midst of an enormous transformation and its final form is not yet clear." Although this article was first published in 2003, it has continued to serve as the clarion call for the HR function to better serve its respective organizations. The HR function has a rich history of transforming itself. From being known as *industrial relations* to *personnel* to *human resource management,* the function has evolved and adapted itself in order to assist organizations in the management of people. This book picks up on this continuous transformation process in an attempt to more clearly define and map out strategies for success in this effort. Many other researchers agree with this need.

The continuing controversy regarding HR's role and relationship with its organization continues. Keith Hammonds (2005, p. 1) states, "Let's face it: after close to 20 years of hopeful rhetoric about becoming 'strategic partners' with 'a seat at the table' where business decisions that matter are made, most human-resources professionals aren't nearly there. They have no seat, and the table is locked in a conference room to which they have no key. HR people are, for most practical purposes, neither strategic nor leaders." Hammonds goes on to give four reasons why the HR function currently fails in the roles of leadership and delivering value to the organization. First, Hammonds says that "HR people aren't the sharpest tacks in the box," explaining that most managers arrive to take on HR duties after having been rated as subpar as managers in other functional disciplines within the organization. Second, he says, "HR pursues efficiency in lieu of value." Not that efficiency is a bad thing. In fact, it is essential to any concern operating in today's highly competitive marketplace. But in addition to controlling costs, the HR function must leverage the activities that it performs into value-driven impact for the organization through its people. Third, Hammonds asserts, "HR isn't working for you" but instead working to cover itself and its practices through standard practices intended for everyone and uniform treatment toward issues that arise from workforce efforts. Fourth, "the corner office doesn't get HR (and vice versa)." In the emergence and continuous evolution of the function, HR has been regarded as a necessary evil. Some would say even an *unnecessary evil*. The foundations of this function bear interest for discussion here.

One important historical figure in this discussion is Peter Drucker, whose death in 2005 at age ninety-five truly marked the end of an era. His influence on modern management was profound. Among the considerable evidence of his influence on HR was the chapter in his classic 1954 book, *The Practice of Management,* titled "Is Personnel Management Bankrupt?" Drucker had the distinction of being among the first to raise an issue that has consistently resurfaced over the past fifty years. That issue centers on the actual and desired role of human resource management (HRM), formerly called personnel administration. Drucker noted in the 1954 book that HR people consistently complain that they are not accorded respect, lack the status they should be given, and are not treated as full-fledged members of senior management.

The issue about which Drucker was writing has evolved into current thinking about HR transformation. *HR transformation* has many possible meanings—and, indeed, may well be a term in search of a definition. But it usually means "a radical effort to change, rethink, reinvent, and reposition HR's role in the organization." Although the direction of that radical rethinking can vary depending on the pressing business needs of the organization in which HR is to be transformed, one way it plays out is to cut a dramatic percentage of HR staff and then force the department to recharter. Rechartering means coming up with a new mission, list of goals, and list of achievable and measurable objectives. Often, a failure in HR transformation can lead to a total outsourcing of the HR function in an organization or, at a minimum, loss of the ability to yield any positive impact on organizational results. Yet beyond such a historical view of the function, current HR professionals share responsibility here as well. The goal of HR transformation is to reposition HR to live up to the great promise it offers to provide leadership on the increasingly important role of human capital in organizations.

Numerous studies have been conducted over the past several years detailing the competencies required of the HR function. These competency studies point out the need for HR to develop areas of expertise, from business knowledge to consulting skills to human capital impact initiatives. Some progress has been made. But more remains to be done if HR practitioners are to exert genuine leadership roles in organizational settings. The future holds much promise for HR professionals who are prepared to do that.

But the HR function and its potential impact on an organization do not have to be stuck in this rut. John Boudreau (Lawler, Boudreau, and Mohrman 2005, p. 3) notes that HR "is a unique organization in the company. It discovers things about the business through the lens of people and talent. That's an opportunity for competitive advantage." To this new viewpoint, the authors believe that the HR function is best poised to add value by transforming itself into the unique alignment of strategy, processes, and transactional services required by its respective organization. Such a transformation requires a redefined leadership perspective. But it should not be transformation for transformation's sake. It should be transformation to create sustainability and to reposition HR to a more strategic and less transactionally oriented, risk-averse, compliance, and bureaucratic mind-set.

This book is intended for those willing to grow, think, and work differently in HR. It is a guide for mapping out a plan of action for aligning and implementing a new agenda for connecting the HR function to the success of the organization. It is intended to be a guide to HR transformation, providing important information about what trends and issues prompt HR transformation, what HR transformation can mean, what business case can be made for that change, how the direction of that change can be established and managed, and how its relative success can be measured.

This book is intended to provide HR leaders with insight into the many possible strategic decisions that they could make. We will talk about these strategic decisions in two contexts: the first is the context of the base organization's fundamental business or operational challenge, the business transformation; and the second is the context of what HR did to adapt, that is, to achieve HR transformation.

This book presents a number of case studies to illustrate how human resource professionals have dealt with the trends affecting their organizations. In each case we will explore the contexts for both business transformation and HR transformation.

The Need for This Book

Organizations have several important reasons to focus attention on HR transformation now. Each relates directly to the need for this book. First, HR transformation can be the focus of total organizational change. After all, the nature of the people in an organization and how they are managed necessarily affects organizational success. That is particularly true in an age of knowledge workers whose intellectual capital influences and increasingly becomes the basis for setting the direction of business and the identification and cultivation of new markets. Second, HR transformation can be a means by which leaders help their organizations become, and remain, competitive amid rapidly changing external environmental conditions. Third, HR transformation can be a focal point for efforts to align all HR initiatives with one another and the HR function itself with the organization's strategic objectives.

The Purpose of the Book

This book is written for HR leaders, though many others—including supervisors, operating managers, and experienced employees—may benefit from it. This book is an action guide that describes how to transform HR. This book can also be used to improve the ways in which current HR practices in an organization support business objectives and the ways in which different HR functional areas support one another.

Overview of the Contents

The book contains eight chapters, which are divided into three parts. Part One is titled "Transforming HR." Chapter 1 lays the book's foundation by defining HR transformation, clarifying the business need for it, and explaining the directions HR transformation often takes. Chapter 2 examines broadly the trends that have influenced the workforce, the workplace, and HR over the past ten years, and how they influenced the need for HR transformation and the need for new roles and approaches for HR professionals.

Part Two is titled "Focusing on Future Trends." Chapter 3 examines the future trends in the workplace and how they affect, or should affect, HR practice. Chapter 4 reviews, in more detail than Chapter 2 did, the future trends in the general workforce and how they affect, or should affect, HR practice. Chapter 5 examines the way to transform HR by focusing on future workforce trends.

Part Three is titled "Enacting a New Role of HR Leadership." Chapter 6 explains what HR leadership means, examining past, present, and future thinking about the role that HR should play in an organization. Chapter 7 examines how to build HR leadership in an organization. And Chapter 8, the final chapter, offers some insights on how to demonstrate HR leadership in the face of outsourcing.

Acknowledgments

···

Writing a book is a real challenge. The challenge is even greater when the authors are in different locations, are busy people, and write in between teaching, training, and consulting engagements.

The authors wish to offer special thanks to their publisher, Davies-Black Publishing, for its support and understanding. Bill Rothwell wishes to thank Lin Gao, his trusted and dedicated graduate research assistant at Penn State, for her help in tracking down the copyright permissions for this book.

Bob Prescott would like to offer special thanks to Julie Barber, Lynda Boyce, Lauren Candito, Robert Etheredge, Dieter Hinrichs, and Katie Phillips for their research efforts. Maria Taylor would like to express her deepest appreciation to the many people who supported this project, especially Rachael Bourque, for her enthusiasm for research and this project; to Jim Kuhn, for many hours of brainstorming, analysis, and inspiration; to her two sons, David and Brendan, for love, support, and many hours of Brendan's diligent proofreading.

About the Authors

....

William J. Rothwell, PhD, SPHR, is a Professor of Workforce Education and Development, part of the Department of Learning and Performance Systems on the University Park campus of the Pennsylvania State University. In that capacity, he leads a graduate specialty in Workplace Learning and Performance. He is also President of his own consulting company, Rothwell & Associates (see www.rothwell-associates.com).

Rothwell completed a BA in English from Illinois State University, an MA (and all courses for the doctorate) in English at the University of Illinois at Urbana-Champaign, an MBA with a specialty in Human Resource Management at Sangamon State University (now the University of Illinois at Springfield), and a PhD in Education/Training at the University of Illinois at Urbana-Champaign. He has also earned life accreditation as a Senior Professional in Human Resources (SPHR) through the Human Resource Certification Institute and earned the Registered Organization Development Consultant (RODC) designation through the Organization Development Institute.

Before entering academe, from 1979 to 1993, Rothwell was a Director of Human Resource Development in the public and private sectors. He managed, planned, designed, and evaluated countless training, HR, and organization development programs.

Rothwell has authored, coauthored, edited, or coedited more than 275 books and articles. Well known for his work in succession planning and talent management, he has recently published the following books: B. Powers and W. Rothwell, *Instructor Excellence: Mastering the Delivery of Training,* 2nd ed. (San Francisco: Pfeiffer, 2007); R. Cecil and W. Rothwell, *Next Generation Management Development: The Complete Guide and Resource* (San Francisco: Pfeiffer, 2007); W. Rothwell, M. Butler, C. Maldonado, D. Hunt, K. Peters, J. Li, and J. Stern, *Handbook of Training Technology: An Introductory Guide to Facilitating Learning with Technology— from Planning Through Evaluation* (San Francisco: Pfeiffer, 2006); W. Rothwell, *Effective Succession Planning: Ensuring Leadership Continuity and Building Talent from Within,* 3rd ed. (New York: Amacom, 2005); W. Rothwell, R. Jackson, S. Knight, and J. Lindholm, *Career Planning and Succession Management: Developing Your Organization's Talent—for Today and Tomorrow* (Westport, CT: Greenwood Press, 2005); W. Rothwell and R. Sullivan (eds.), *Practicing Organization Development: A Guide for Consultants,* 2nd ed. (San Francisco: Pfeiffer, 2005); W. Rothwell and H. Kazanas, *Strategic Planning for Human Resources* (Mumbai, India: Jaico Publishing House, 2005); and W. Rothwell, *Beyond Training and Development: The Groundbreaking Classic,* 2nd ed. (New York: Amacom, 2005).

He can be reached at wjr9@psu.edu.

Robert K. Prescott, PhD, SPHR, is Associate Professor of Management at the Crummer Graduate School of Business at Rollins College in Winter Park, Florida. In this role, he is responsible for teaching graduate-level courses in both the MBA and MHR programs.

Formerly, Prescott was the Executive Director of Management and Executive Education at Rollins College; Director of the Management Development Institute and Adjunct Faculty at Eckerd College, an affiliate of the Center for Creative Leadership, in St. Petersburg, Florida; Director of Executive Education and Corporate Services and Instructor at the Pennsylvania State University, University Park, Pennsylvania; and Director of Human Resources for BellSouth Communications, in Birmingham, Alabama. In this corporate management role, he was responsible for all facets of people management practices. Most important, he played a strategic role in representing the human resource function in overall company planning and operations.

His personal teaching expertise and research focus on human resource management, organization behavior, training and development, and consulting. He has taught in formal classroom and executive education settings at the University of Alabama, the University of Alberta-Canada, Cornell University, Eckerd College, the University of Minnesota, the Pennsylvania State University, Wilfred Laurier University-Canada, and Rollins College.

Prescott has personally worked with such companies as the American Automobile Association, American Sales, Bermuda Employers' Council, Conoco, Deloitte & Touche, Delphi Automotive Systems, Estée Lauder, the Internal Revenue Service, Lockheed Martin EIS, Merrill Lynch, the National Basketball Association (NBA), Olive Garden Restaurants, PR Newswire, Scholastic Books, T-Mobile, Walt Disney World, the United Nations World Food Programme, and the U.S. Army.

Prescott, a native of Birmingham, Alabama, holds a BS in Marketing from the University of Alabama and a PhD in Workforce Education and Development from the Pennsylvania State University. He serves on the Board of Directors of the Human Resource Planning Society (HRPS) and most recently was cochair of the National Conference for HRPS. He also serves on the Cornell University ILR Board of Advisors, the Board of Directors for the Conference on Management and Executive Development, and the Board of Directors for Correct Craft. He is a member of the Society for Human Resource Management and the American Society for Training and Development. Prescott is a graduate of the Human Resource Executive Program at Penn State University and is a life-certified Senior Professional in Human Resources (SPHR). He coauthored the book *The Strategic Human Resource Leader: How to Prepare Your Organization for the 6 Key Trends Shaping the Future* (Mountain View, CA: Davies-Black Publishing, 1998).

Prescott can be reached by phone at 407-646-2593 and by e-mail at rprescott@rollins.edu.

Maria Taylor is a Director of Learning Solutions for Raytheon Professional Services. She leads account teams in new-client development and the design and execution of innovative solutions to deliver workforce performance on critical business success factors such as speed to market, customer satisfaction, and cost reduction. Raytheon Professional Services, a global leader in learning services and outsourcing, serves learners in seventy countries and delivers more than seven million hours of training annually to clients who desire innovative solutions that integrate business strategy, human resource development, talent management, and learning. Her recent engagements include building integrated enterprise-wide learning systems to support strategic imperatives and competency-based talent development needs, new product launch, organizational transformation of sales and customer service, executive development to support double-digit profitable growth, competency-based leadership development, and total learning outsourcing.

Prior to joining Raytheon in August 2000, Taylor was the Managing Director of Executive Education for the Smeal College of Business Administration at the Pennsylvania State University. She was responsible for client development, program design, and overall operations and profitability of Penn State's top-ranked global executive education programs. In this capacity, she worked with client organizations in the Global 500, government, and the military.

Taylor was also a Vice President in the banking industry with responsibility for client development, credit underwriting, and relationship management of a full range of credit, cash management, and investment services in the corporate, commercial, and retail sectors of the banking industry.

Taylor coauthored *The Strategic Human Resource Leader: How to Prepare Your Organization for the 6 Key Trends Shaping the Future* (Mountain View, CA: Davies-Black Publishing, 1998). She has published articles and papers in the *Journal of Higher Education, Journal of Management Development,* and through the Institute for the Study of Organizational Effectiveness.

Taylor received a BA in Political Science and an MBA in Finance from the Pennsylvania State University. She has recently served on the Board of Directors for the Louisiana Council for Manufacturing Sciences and the Planning Committee for the Human Resources Planning Society 2004 Annual Conference. She is a member of the Society for Human Resource Management and the Learning Innovation Laboratory at Harvard.

Part One

Transforming HR

1

What Is Human Resource Transformation?

....

Human resource transformation has seized the imagination of operating managers and HR practitioners alike. HR transformation is about reinventing, reconceptualizing, and rechartering what HR is—without assuming that HR is or should be "what we have always done in HR," "what everyone else is doing in HR," or "what appears in standardized HR college textbooks." It means more than just applying technology to HR, containing the costs of HR, reducing the ratio of HR staff to organizational employees, or outsourcing HR activities (Lawler et al., 2004), although these efforts may play a part in a strategic review of HR's purpose in an organization (Christensen 2005; Fischer 2003; Reddington, Williamson, and Withers 2005). A 2006 survey of one hundred large employers revealed that the key business drivers for HR transformation include (1) attracting, retaining, and growing talent (67 percent); (2) supporting the business by focusing HR on core capabilities (47 percent); and (3) supporting business changes (41 percent) (Miller 2006). Other drivers exist, of course, though those listed are representative of many of the most common ones.

Consider each of the following expressions of views that demonstrate the need for HR transformation:

- "We need HR to become more strategic in its emphasis," noted the chief executive officer (CEO) of a large company. "I, for one, would like to see HR take more of a role in managing change and in organization development."

- "Our managers really need help in dealing with the day-to-day—as well as strategic—people problems and challenges they face," noted the HR manager of a small industrial plant. "Even a Harvard MBA does not do justice to the challenges of managing people that our managers face. And if talented people make the key competitive difference between most organizations, then our managers need more help in managing talent. HR should adopt a role more as performance consultants to help managers meet this challenge."

- "The real problem today," said one consultant, "is corruption and ethical problems. In a post-Enron world with the severe restrictions of the Sarbanes-Oxley Act imposed on businesses, HR managers must become the ethics cops to prevent ethical, legal, and moral violations from occurring in companies. In today's world, HR must be the arbiter of ethics. Without some part of the organization playing that role, corruption problems—particularly in some portion of the globe—will only intensify."

Defining HR Transformation

HR transformation does not have one universal definition. It is not a trademarked term. Each organization and its leaders must define what this change effort means to them, why they wish to undertake it, and what results they seek from it. But one thing is clear: demands on HR are changing, as are expectations about the competencies required of HR practitioners (Claus and Collison 2004).

The Drivers and Barriers for HR Transformation

Human resources is a function in the organization that managers and workers do not always appreciate. Consequently, there is sometimes dissatisfaction with what HR is and does. Key drivers for HR transformation, according to a 2005 survey (Rampat 2005, p. 7) include the following:

- Making HR strategic (68 percent)
- Improving service (66 percent)
- Responding to changes in business (60 percent)
- Benefiting from new technology (49 percent)
- Better managing the cost of internal processes (47 percent)

The same survey also revealed the following key barriers to the success of HR transformation:

- Lack of appropriate skills among HR staff
- Lack of appropriate support technology
- An unwillingness to take risk or deal with complexity
- Difficulties in dealing with bureaucracy
- Difficulties in dealing with corporate or international cultural differences
- Lack of employee buy-in to HR transformation
- Failure in building the business case to support the change
- Lack of genuine top management support
- Regulatory constraints
- Unions

Of course, these same issues may also be barriers to many other organizational change efforts.

The real issue here is that too many organizational leaders—and HR professionals—do not question why HR exists and do not clarify what they want from it and how that can be achieved. Traditional actions by HR practitioners and traditional expectations for the HR function by line managers and other stakeholders sometimes interact to create conditions for the failure of the HR function. These problems can be classified into several common complaints about traditional HR practices and into several specific problematic roles thrust upon HR practitioners. Both are worthy of review because they help shed light on the need for a new way of thinking about the HR function.

Complaints about the HR function and about HR practitioners abound in many organizations. Some are reflected in the expressions of views at the beginning of this chapter. Others can be heard when talking to CEOs or line managers in organizations large and small, and in all sectors of the U.S. economy. (Different complaints are heard about HR practices in other nations, of course.) The authors of this book believe that five such complaints are most common:

1. *HR practitioners do not possess a sufficient working knowledge of what business is all about or of the strategic goals of the organization they serve.* This impression can be created, for example, by overzealous HR practitioners who push a presumably social agenda without taking time to show how such efforts will help their organizations meet business needs and achieve strategic objectives. The resulting impression is that HR practitioners care less about business results than others do.

2. *HR practitioners lack leadership ability.* This is particularly true when HR practitioners lack line management experience and are perceived to be less interested in helping line managers solve their problems with people and more interested in meeting the "professional" goals of the HR effort and/or ensuring organizational compliance with governmental laws and regulations or organizational policies and procedures.

3. *HR practitioners are reactive.* Suppose, for instance, that line managers want to install team-based management. Traditional HR practices that reward individual contributors do not work well in conjunction with team-based management. HR practitioners who defend the old system without offering assistance in adapting HR practices to support the new system are (not surprisingly) regarded as reactively focused. They appear unresponsive—and even resistant—to line management's needs, interests, and business pressures.

4. *HR practitioners are sometimes seen as unable to take the lead to establish a vision for change and garner the support necessary to lead the charge.* When top managers hand them the responsibility to spearhead a new effort—such as starting up a process improvement effort, a reengineering initiative, a talent management program, or a "balanced scorecard" approach—then the ability of HR to lead the initiative is showcased. But HR practitioners who cannot successfully implement such an effort lose respect and credibility.

5. *HR practitioners are fad chasers who want to find solutions to problems in other organizations and then "drop them in place"*—without taking into account the unique business objectives, corporate culture, organization-specific politics, and individual personalities of key decision makers found in their own organizational settings.

Think about your own organization. How much would the HR function be accused—rightfully or not—of such problems? If in doubt, ask some line managers, individually, for their opinions. If any agree with one or more of these problems with the HR function, then ask for a story based on the individual's experience that illustrates the problem. Such information can be valuable in identifying key strategic weaknesses of the HR function in one organizational context. Keep the results of this exercise in mind as you read this book so that you can pinpoint key areas of priority and can develop plans to change the HR function in your organization.

Not all HR problems are caused by HR practitioners themselves, as the previous description of complaints about HR may imply. Sometimes HR practitioners are the victims of wrongheaded expectations by top managers, middle managers, and even employees. The result is that HR is thrust into problematic or dubious roles. Such roles may include the following:

- Traffic cop
- Enforcer
- Line management gopher
- Scapegoat
- Paper-shuffling bureaucrat (Rothwell, Prescott, and Taylor 1998b)

The *traffic cop role* has an obvious meaning. On occasion, HR practitioners are expected to "chase down offenders of governmental or organizational policy" and "give them a warning." Although some HR practitioners are all too willing to play this role, others know that it gives the impression that the HR function is interested only in compliance and not in results.

The *enforcer role* in HR is related to that of a traffic cop. When "offenders" against governmental or organizational policy go too far, someone is expected to take action and punish them. Many executives are loathe to "play the bad guy" and thus prefer to delegate such bothersome chores. Who better than HR practitioners to serve this role? Like members of a Mob hit squad, HR practitioners are expected to move beyond the role of traffic cop to play judge, jury, and (metaphorical) executioner with those who transgress rules.

When cast in the *line management gopher role,* HR practitioners are expected to take action on behalf of busy top managers. Often this happens whenever the word *people* is used by some managers, because they are all too eager to hand the job over to the HR function. In fact, some managers think they should delegate the handling of all their people issues to HR practitioners, just as they would like to hand over all their accounting problems to the accounting department or all their purchasing problems to the purchasing department. The problem with this logic is, of course, that managing people cannot be separated from the manager's job. Rather than partner with HR, these managers want to dump their people problems on HR practitioners—and blame HR practitioners when the problems are not fixed quickly enough or are not fixed properly.

The *scapegoat role* casts the HR function as a loser. It is all too often a thankless job, a no-win situation. Whenever a new mandate to jump on the latest bandwagon is handed down by corporate headquarters, top managers who lack commitment to the effort want to shove the job of handling it onto the HR function. This sets up HR practitioners for failure, of course. This is especially true when top or middle managers have no interest in, or support for, the new mandate; have not clarified the results the organization wants from the effort or why it is wanted; or don't know how the new effort will be measured. The real test of commitment to the mandate is to find out how much time, money, and personal attention the CEO is willing to give an effort. If the CEO is unwilling to personally support a new mandate, then it is a surefire sign that the HR function is being set up as scapegoat. If the initiative fails, the top managers can claim it failed abysmally due to the unconscionable mishandling of HR practitioners. (Of course, forward-thinking CEOs view the HR function in a different way.) Unwilling to challenge senior executives, some HR practitioners are all too eager to carry out this dubious role, thinking it will help them curry favor with the organization's leaders.

Finally, HR practitioners are sometimes cast in the *paper-shuffling bureaucrat role*. From the earliest days, the HR function has been responsible for keeping records to satisfy government or legal reporting requirements. One reason that HR departments were founded—and that some exist to this day—is to maintain a paper trail to satisfy government requirements. Often that just means shuffling useless paper. Of course, information technology has led to more records, though they are stored electronically rather than manually. Some otherwise excellent HR practitioners are reduced to playing the role of paper-shuffling bureaucrats because that is all they are permitted to do or because that is all that is desired of them. Some managers have the wrongheaded notion that this role is the only one HR practitioners could play.

A Brief Overview of the Historical Evolution of the HR Field

To understand why the HR function needs HR transformation in the future, it is useful to consider HR's background. This section briefly describes the evolution of the HR field—where it has been and where it is now, drawing from Rothwell, Prescott, and Taylor (1998b).

The Past: Where Has the HR Field Been?

The evolution of the human resource management (HRM) field, once called *personnel,* has followed the history of business in the United States. As the Industrial Revolution swept the United States in the nineteenth century, rapidly growing organizations faced three major people-related challenges: (1) managing sudden and massive increases in the size of the workforce stemming from industrialization, (2) fighting workforce unionization, and (3) integrating the huge influx of immigrant workers into U.S. workplaces.

From the dawn of the Industrial Revolution in the United States until about 1950, the personnel department's role in most organizations centered around administrative duties. Personnel directors headed up a record-keeping function, which included such activities as disciplinary systems, recruitment, safety programs, time-and-motion studies, and union relations. Senior managers expected that these personnel activities would maintain employee morale and enhance cooperation within their organizations.

From the 1940s into the 1950s, personnel departments emphasized their role in meeting employee needs to achieve economic security. During this time, unions were responsible for negotiating wages and other employee benefits such as pension plans and health insurance. Corporate personnel departments were founded in the late 1950s to coordinate such increasingly specialized functions as benefits, wages, recruitment, and labor relations. During that time the evolution of functionally specific personnel departments occurred.

The business and social dynamics of the 1960s and 1970s brought increased attention within the personnel department to human relations. Human relations emphasized supervisory training, which often included role-playing and sensitivity training as well as participative management techniques such as management by objectives (MBO) and quality circles (QC). As one consequence of focusing on human relations, personnel departments were eventually handed responsibility for training and development, reward systems, performance management systems, and succession planning programs. At the same time, personnel departments also assumed responsibilities to help their organizations meet new challenges stemming from increasing government laws, rules, and regulations affecting (among other areas) equal employment opportunity, occupational safety and health, and employee benefits.

The transformation of personnel management to human resource management was affected by a parallel trend: the emergence of the human resource development (HRD) field from the training and development field. HRD prompted a fresh look at the importance of developing people and forced a reconceptualization of how that is done by introducing a conceptual umbrella covering employee training, education, and development. The shift taking place in HRM, apparent in the early 1980s, may have resulted from the convergence of traditional personnel specialists with HRD practitioners. At that point personnel officially became human resource management to reflect its emphasis on employees as valued organizational resources.

The Present: Where Is the HR Field Now?

In organizations at present, the HR function provides essential services to such stakeholders as job applicants, employees, supervisors, middle managers, and executives. However, the HR function tends to be positioned at the end of the business process chain—on the reactive side—and too often focuses on carrying out activities rather than achieving results. The HR function's role is currently one of providing people, training, and isolated HR efforts after others have formulated organizational strategy and have initiated operational implementation.

HR practitioners in recent years have been driven by events in their organizations to direct attention to such issues as downsizing, outplacement, retraining, diversity, employee rights, technology's effects on people, and recruiting skilled talent at a time of expected labor shortages and record employment. Cost-focused management of employee benefits programs such as health insurance, workers compensation, and pension plans has also figured prominently in an effort to control skyrocketing expenses. Among other HR issues of interest at present are alternatives to litigation, diversity, the Employee Retirement Income Security Act (ERISA), family and medical leave issues, employee handbooks, policies and procedures manuals, employee privacy, sexual harassment avoidance, use of temporary workers, and workforce reductions.

Building organizational capability is a primary focus of HR organizations. *Organizational capability*, defined in the simplest terms, is linked to what an organization must do to act on its strategies. Those capabilities must be identified, developed, and then measured by comparing current workforce performance to business goals. The key to this performance rests in the hands of people. Never before have HR practitioners been challenged to do so much. Ironically, this is happening at precisely the time when HR wages are not growing as fast as they once did and when many HR functions have lost staff members in recent downsizings.

The HR function is also required—more than ever before—to align and integrate its efforts in relation to organizational goals. Linking HR strategy and business strategy has become a major preoccupation for HR practitioners today. The HR field has evolved from an activity-focused to a strategy-focused effort.

Case Studies on HR Transformation

We can learn from reviewing case studies in HR transformation. As you read the following case studies, think about what they have in common as well as how they differ. Note that HR transformation does not mean just one thing. It has many possible meanings, depending on the business and the HR objectives. Also read, at the end of this chapter, the Transformation in Action example "The Future of HR—Think Bigger!" for a description of what HR transformation means to Linda Merritt at AT&T.

Case Study 1
Reengineering HR Delivery at IBM

Faced with declining revenues and significant business losses in the early 1990s, IBM reviewed its products, services, infrastructure, operations, and functions. (For more on this case study, see "Re-engineering HR Delivery at IBM" 2002.) As part of this process, IBM either reformed or eliminated HR processes, policies, and practices.

Bob Gonzales, vice president of HR operations and founding director of IBM's National Human Resources Service Center (NHRSC), which emerged as a far-reaching development in reengineering HR, recalls, "We had this bold vision of an ongoing journey, which, by transforming HR, could also revitalize the business. It was a strategic change of the highest order." HR was restructured into a stand-alone service business with regional centers and small staffs at IBM locations in the United States. Then consolidated service centers were created for HR, with its information technology (IT) requirements organized around service processes with technology-leveraged delivery. Later, the NHRSC was launched in Raleigh, North Carolina, to deliver information to IBM managers, employees, and pensioners in the United States, using network technologies. The use of technology released HR specialists to provide higher-level HR support and value.

IBM's HR, as it is today, was realized by two further developments: the full merging of all HR information systems with NHRSC and the establishment of a virtual network of HR partner teams to serve line and business-unit customers.

The service center was the catalyst for HR transformation. Incorporating the best of call-center practice, along with leading-edge technology for self-service, it improved IBM's productivity, reduced costs, and gained customer (i.e., employee) satisfaction with what HR provided and how those services were performed. Successive annual cost reductions of 30 percent, 10 percent, 15 percent, and 8 percent were achieved as new programs were added. As Gonzales says, "The center has surpassed our expectations. It is a classic example of an idea and solution well beyond its time and the norm for HR service delivery. It opened completely new perspectives for us on the future of HR."

Originally established as a benefits center, IBM's NHRSC today makes the best use of technology, information, and processes for its four hundred staff to deliver twenty-two programs—from employee benefits to workforce diversity and from staffing to management development. The service center serves a total IBM population of 625,000, including managers, employees, spouses, dependents, and pensioners. The center receives around 1.7 million calls a year, deals with more than 1 million reports or queries, and conducts 3.4 million online transactions. It processes nearly 700,000 job applications, surveys the attitudes of 188,000 employees, and receives more than 10,000 ideas for consideration. More than a quarter of contacts made to the center are resolved automatically by voice response unit (VRU) technology. Benefits enrollment and changes in personal data are examples.

After the self-service stage, the center is backed by three tiers of staff who respond to the calls not answered by VRU: (1) customer-service representatives or HR generalists, who are an initial point of contact to provide first-level problem solving and transaction processing; (2) HR subject-matter specialists for issue resolution, plan and program interpretation, and advanced expertise, handling less than 20 percent of the calls received; and (3) at the top tier, HR program experts, who serve in a design, research, policy, strategy, and external-benchmarking capacity.

Self-service applications and the consultancy and advisory work of the national HR service center are two channels of IBM's HR service-delivery model. A third is the network of 150 "HR partners" who work with line managers at IBM manufacturing, sales, service, and field locations throughout the USA. Their responsibilities include the following:

- Providing strategic and operational support on HR programs and policies to assigned line managers

- Influencing decisions made by senior management

- Leading HR program implementation

- Developing new unit HR programs in support of line management

Examples of HR partner inputs include training and updating executives in HR programs and policies, helping to implement pension-plan changes, guiding local managers in applying the performance-management system to compensation, and helping to build positive employee relations with line managers. Gonzales explains, "They are doers, facilitators, co-coordinators and leaders for the organizations to which they are attached, who leverage a unit's skills and people resources to best effect to resolve their internal clients' business issues and needs." In these services, however, a partner will not necessarily have to act alone.

According to Gonzales, "Partners, designers, and experts act as one borderless team through virtual relationships and are successful, because we have never lost sight of our HR objectives. Through low-cost, high-quality services and continuous process implementation, we can deliver workplace and customer satisfaction."

The more that transactional services are provided electronically, the greater the opportunities for HR personnel to deliver higher-level business consultancy and advice to line management. Gonzales' target for the latter is to do so with a 1,000:1 line to HR-partner ratio, which aims to optimize the effectiveness of the partner network in the United States. He realizes, too, that reskilling HR people will continue to be an issue and that fewer HR staff may be required in the future.

"Our ambition is to achieve a global e-HR capability with one database for all employees worldwide, but we are only at the tip of the iceberg as yet," says Gonzales. Technological advances lag in some regions, and language is a problem in others. His vision is of virtual HR teams operating globally. Two fledgling groups, global e-business and global performance management, are beginning to produce results, although huge challenges remain.

But Bob Gonzales also knows that communication and recognition of accomplishments are central to success among the HR population. "We anticipated the tremendous communication efforts required to reinforce crucial messages and deliberately celebrated our wins whenever they occurred," he said. "Both were key to building HR satisfaction in the journey to internal customer satisfaction."

···

···

Case Study 2
Strategic Change and HR Alignment at Reliant Energy

Reliant Energy, Inc., of Houston, Texas, has tackled difficult regulatory, competitive, structural, and cultural issues successfully through transforming its human resource management function and processes. (For more on this case study, see "Strategic Change and HR Alignment at Reliant Energy" 2001.) Design and implementation of a strategic-alignment model have been of critical importance, along with high-impact practices in recruitment, retention, total rewards, application of technology, and measurement of competitive performance.

No matter what they have already achieved, even the best HR people need to be reenergized, stimulated intellectually, and guided to understand where they are against world-class best practice. Houston-based Reliant Energy hired management thinker Dave Ulrich to address all its HR specialists on the state of best practice and, a year later, engaged James Walker, founder of the U.S.-based Walker Group and one of the foremost emerging HR authorities, to help HR to assess itself against leading organizations.

Reliant has an eighty-six-person-strong corporate HR team, plus more than thirty other professionals in field locations. Alan P. Warnick ("Strategic Change" 2001), director of organizational effectiveness, explains: "It's a long-distance race without end because reassessing, benchmarking, and renewing HR is a constant process. We always have to ask what is a better—or the best—way?" The "best way" for Warnick and his team over time has involved repositioning the function, reengineering HR processes, streamlining service delivery, transferring people's accountabilities, and implementing high-impact practices. But the HR function's most enduring achievement over the past three years, Warnick says, has been a self-devised model for the strategic alignment of people practices in the organization. This is followed closely by Reliant's annual competitive-performance index, an employee survey that has become a U.S. benchmark for culture change, and the company's technology-enabled total-rewards Web site, a self-service work-life facility for employees to raise any queries or input changes in detail.

The six-step strategic-alignment model ties HR irrevocably to corporate and strategic business-unit strategies and gives both the organization and the HR function a rapid-response capability to whatever the business environment throws at Reliant. Aside from drivers such as regulation, technology, and economics, other challenges come from competitors, ever-selective customers, or from supplier and business-partner relationships. The business environment represents the model's first step.

Taking these factors into account and forecasting their potential changes over one- to five-year timescales enables leaders to set—or amend, if need be—the business vision. This vision is the second step, which attempts to define what the organization's future image and characteristics will have to be when operating at full potential. Clarity at this level shapes appropriate strategies for the short- to long-term actions required to accomplish the vision, strategies that make up step three. The process so far provides the context for the strategic alignment of HR, which leads to three further steps that need to be undertaken:

- Review of business capabilities required to fulfill strategies—organizational, strategic-marketing, technological, financial, and economic

- Review of workforce competencies—the critical knowledge, technical expertise, skills, and behaviors that build capabilities

- Review of high-impact practices in HR strategy, structure, processes, people, and total rewards

Constructing the model for the company was an iterative process supported by benchmarking with leading companies, organization-wide participation in design and implementation, communication, modification after evaluating its effectiveness and, naturally, executive sponsorship. The model was designed on-site, although it was guided by, among other influences, J. Galbraith's thinking on his "star" model in *Designing Organizations* (2001). Warnick explains,

> According to our thinking, new talent—often younger people and graduates—does not want to work for stodgy, rigid organizations, which raises structural issues like image and flexibility. Add the personal expectations of this new generation of workers—freedom to do things their way, opportunities to progress, appropriate rewards, a challenging environment, a work-life balance and so on—and HR processes become crucial enablers of capability development.

> In this scenario, business conditions and people expectations therefore create a need for what we call 'employment appropriateness,' which is of strategic importance because talented people nowadays will not stay put if they do not receive it. This issue is becoming more intense and, for many organizations, requires a big leap into reality if they are to avoid very high replacement costs or downtime in productivity and performance.

Warnick's reference to today's context for HR highlights why Reliant reengineered its core HR processes as the basis for designing and implementing high-impact people practices. "Doing so seeks to achieve a stronger competitive performance for the business, and a means of reinforcing our desired culture," he adds.

Over time, Reliant has had to almost continuously rethink its culture and behaviors in response to external events. Once a hierarchical, bureaucratic electric utility, the deregulation of the U.S. energy industry required a shift in the company's culture, as did the 1996 acquisition of Noram, which brought with it six thousand new employees. The total workforce of Reliant now numbers about thirteen thousand.

The key issues for Warnick and colleagues are culture assessment, development, and—in the case of the Noram acquisition—merging of cultures, since more opportunities of this kind might occur in the future. In fact, after due-diligence reviews, Warnick's ongoing priority in this area is to decide which HR practices will help meld Reliant's and

Noram's respective approaches to people management, getting work done, decision making, and so on.

Warnick advises that "renewing HR and making continuous contributions to strategy and competitive performance are not a linear, or single, task. You have to move ahead on several fronts simultaneously to achieve the greatest impacts, guided by honest responses to one question, 'What is the best way?'"

Beyond Scorecards

These case studies demonstrate that HR transformation takes many forms. HR transformation is often a means to an end of organizational transformation. As is also clear from the case studies and from writings on HR transformation, measuring HR processes has become a major point of focus in many organizations. Although each HR function— such as training, recruitment, selection, compensation, or benefits— lends itself to unique measurements, thought leaders of HR are also suggesting that HR itself should be assessed by a strategic scorecard to indicate how well HR functions such as training and recruitment work harmoniously together (horizontal alignment) and contribute to achieving the organization's strategic objectives (vertical alignment).

But what is needed is not so much a preoccupation with measurement as is a preoccupation with setting measurable goals and then following through to achieve them. In short, measurement is a means to an end. The end is to link up HR, HR functions, individuals, and organizations to achieve balanced and well-formulated results. HR transformation contributes to achieving this challenge. Hence, HR practitioners must think beyond scorecards (how things are measured) to the goals and objectives of HR (what is measured and why).

The Focus of Subsequent Chapters and Questions Considered

This book is all about how to transform HR, realizing the promise of HR transformation to reinvent HR in order to help shape corporate strategy by the strategic alignment of talent with corporate goals.

Chapter 2 focuses on trends influencing the workforce, the workplace, and HR that shape the direction of HR transformation. The key topics treated in the chapter include the following:

- How do trends influence HR and organizations?
- What have been recent key trends, and how have they changed in the past decade?
- How do trends relate to HR transformation?
- How do different stakeholder groups regard HR, and why are their evaluations important?

Chapter 3 describes transforming HR by focusing on future workplace trends. Key topics treated in the chapter include the following:

- What are the key future workplace trends?
- What themes underlie the trends?
- What are the likely impacts of the trends?
- How should the impacts of the trends be managed?
- What do the trends mean for HR transformation?

Chapter 4 is about transforming HR by focusing on future workforce trends. It identifies two key HR trends and addresses such issues as these:

- What themes underlie the trends?
- What are the likely impacts of the trends?
- How should the impacts of the trends be managed?
- What do the trends mean for HR transformation?

Chapter 5 centers on transforming HR by focusing on future HR trends. It addresses such key questions as these:

- What are the key future HR trends?
- What causes the HR trends?
- What are the likely impacts of the HR trends?
- How should the impacts of the HR trends be managed?
- What do these trends mean for HR transformation?

Chapter 6 is about what HR leadership means. It explores such questions as these:

- What is HR leadership?
- How is HR leadership related to HR transformation?
- Who demonstrates HR leadership?
- What should chief people officers do?
- What are the international differences in leadership?
- What are the ethical dilemmas of leadership?

Chapter 7 examines how to build HR leadership in your organization. It considers such questions as these:

- What is needed to diffuse HR leadership throughout the organization?
- How can the whole HR function be involved?
- How are role perceptions of HR managed—and changed?

Chapter 8 describes how to demonstrate HR leadership in the face of outsourcing. A popular way of repositioning—or even radically rethinking and transforming HR—outsourcing is an important issue to consider in HR transformation. This chapter thus addresses critical questions such as these:

- Why do organizations outsource?
- Why do organizations outsource HR functions?
- Why do organizations outsource the entire HR function?
- What are the issues associated with outsourcing?
- What makes human resource outsourcing successful?

The Future of HR—Think Bigger!
Linda Merritt, HR Director, AT&T

In her capacity as HR director for AT&T, Linda Merrit is in the midst of an HR transformation in that organization. In this Transformation Example, she describes what she believes is needed to transform HR.

Before HR can complete the current journey of becoming a strategic business partner, it needs to think even bigger and reach farther—and do it faster.

The business environment is increasingly competitive on a global scale, with dramatic evolution in technology and increased competition and risk literally changing how business is conducted. The speed of innovation and invention and the shift to decrease the cost of production fuels a need for business intelligence on how to best leverage all of the sources of human capital a company can access. This is the realm of human capital management (HCM), and it is more than HR with a new name. HR as we know it remains at the heart, but there is more, much more. In moving from human resources to human capital management, our profession must become a decision science in the same way that finance and marketing have.

The decision science component of HCM uses business and work-force intelligence to inform strategic decision making and allocation of resources to optimally leverage people and their ideas to achieve the goals of the business.

Business intelligence requires data mining, metrics, and analytics. HR swims in data but is too often considered the weakest function in terms of understanding and producing analytics at the business-impact level. We must go way, way beyond turnover, time to hire, and cost per employee.

Whether you upgrade an internal HR technology infrastructure or engage in comprehensive platform outsourcing, you must design (and invest in) the diagnostic capabilities to identify, analyze, and measure issues, impacts, and performance of the enterprise's use of its human capital. And you must monitor external trends in how value is produced through people and their ideas in a globally linked world of complex network business relationships.

Human capital strategy begins with the business strategy for growth. How will the business grow through the acquisition and leverage of human capital—people and their ideas? The employee-based workforce is now only one option of many. You might start with a flexible workforce that includes permanent, temporary, and contract labor. Then consider the expanding human capital supply chain. If you are going to offshore, should you establish "captive centers" or outsource? Should mergers or acquisitions be considered for more than an expanded footprint? If so, how will you manage and measure the integration, retention, and leverage of the human capital initially and over time?

Strategy is only as valuable as the results produced. HCM must deliver results across the expanded definition of *workforce.* How will we redefine workforce management when brand- and revenue-impacting customer contacts are increasingly supported by nonemployees? For example, the new HCM work includes influencing external sourcing contracting and management to address the vendor's training, turnover, incentive transparency, and service levels. If a telemarketer's employees make bad sales in your name, it is your company's brand reputation that will suffer. In telecommunications this is called *slamming,* and it is your company that will be in the news and paying the fines to state regulatory agencies.

If your vendor for customer care has poor training and high turnover, it is your company's customers who will be dissatisfied and perhaps lost. In business process outsourcing (BPO) you are buying performance and results. True, you are not managing the vendor's processes, but you do need to know that its managers are!

HR at its best brings perspective and subject matter expertise that are different from and value added compared with the other business functions. There is more to leveraging human capital than we have space to address here, but I would like to touch on an important area that supports our expanded role—corporate governance.

We have seen what happens when corporate governance is subverted to the service of the current executive suite rather than the business, its employees, and shareholders. Enron, Accenture, and WorldCom are big names that have fallen far and hard. Although only a few senior leaders are found guilty in a court of law, and fewer still go to jail, many more pay the price of the fallen. Losses of jobs, retirement funds, and investments have impacted tens of thousands. Thankfully, company-destroying executive errancy is rare. Yet we already have the much broader scandal of selectively dated stock options and grants. Hundreds of companies are in jeopardy, and several executives have stepped down. Increasing scrutiny is being placed on the role and actions of boards of directors. We must also bring scrutiny and soul searching within our profession about our role in corporate governance.

Structuring the board and senior leadership team, defining management roles and responsibilities, developing total executive compensation packages and employment contracts—these are among the most powerful domains of HR. Advising on the very structure of the business to determine alignment with the goals of the business should be provided by the HR leaders—someone who is there to see the game plan played in real life—and not by consultants who advise and walk away.

Governance matters, and values matter. HR alone will not make a corporation and its senior leaders act ethically, legally, and in favor of the corporation's customers, employees, and investors. But a better balance of internal power and controls at the c-level (the highest executive level) and with the board of directors is needed. Part of that balance could be achieved by adding a chief human capital officer, backed by a professional body of ethics and standards that are enforced by laws and regulations.

We also need to move faster in our transformation. Parts of HR are rapidly being outpaced and displaced by the forces of technology and outsourcing. Technology solutions, software, and Internet-based employee self-services and manager self-services are eliminating paper forms and HR administrators. Remote call centers and 24-7 Web-based applications are displacing the friendly local HR partner—the one that used to be down the hall.

Centralized shared services and outsourcing have been a growing part of HR for some time because of the advantages in costs and services. For years, companies have chosen the services of subject matter experts in areas such as pensions, 401(k) plans, health care claims, and other benefits plan administration services that demand legal and regulatory expertise. Employees get increased access and information, and employers gain a partner in compliance risk management and cost control. Outsourcing the back office—such as payroll, IT operations, and even vendor management of your other vendors—is increasingly common.

Outsourcing is growing and will continue to grow into more and more front office areas of HR. Mega-HRO vendors offer multifunction HR services, from employee call centers to emerging services in recruiting, compensation, and learning.

Removing administrative work unmasks the actual state of HR's strategic and HCM competencies. More available time does not make us strategic business partners. Every HR team on this journey needs the same level of workforce planning as we offer our clients. How will we reskill our teams? What are the new competency models? What is our bench strength and state of succession planning? Who will be able to develop new capabilities, and where will we need to acquire new talent?

The key to the impact of technology and outsourcing on the future of HR is who is driving the decisions and why. If decisions are piecemeal and tactical and are made under financial pressure to increase efficiency, lower costs, and reduce staff, I worry that technology and outsourcing could shrink the scope and value of the HR profession. To the extent that these tools are selected by HR in the context of a strategic plan that enables HR to provide increased value-added, business impacting results and improved employee services at reduced cost, they will be pillars of support for the transformation of HR into human capital management.

2

Recent Influences on the Workforce, the Workplace, and HR

This chapter examines the recent trends that have influenced organizations and shaped the direction of HR transformation. We will examine the following:

- How do trends influence HR and organizations?
- What have been recent key trends, and how have they changed in the past decade?
- How do trends relate to HR transformation?
- How do different stakeholder groups regard HR, and why are their evaluations important?

How Do Trends Influence HR and Organizations?

Our fundamental premise is that the success of a human resource group is ultimately defined by the success of the organization. For corporations, success is defined as satisfied customers and shareholder value.

For health care providers, success is good care for patients, satisfied staff, and a fiscally sound organization. For government, success is effective programs and fiscal prudence. Every organization's leaders face the challenges of how to create value; how to provide the best services, products, and outcomes for the organization's customers, constituents, members, citizens, and patients; how to operate with the most effective and efficient use of resources in the face of changes, obstacles, and competition; and how to survive for the long term. To meet these challenges, human resource leaders must understand the influences that shape their environments and the impact on the organizations, marketplace, and the people they serve. The need for human resource transformation originates from changes in the competitive environment and changes in the organization's strategy and business model as well as from the advance in the practice of human resources. Savvy human resource leaders also examine how others have dealt with these trends, successfully and unsuccessfully, and craft the lessons learned into ideas that can be applied to their own challenges.

The essence of an organization's success is its ability to create and sustain competitive advantage by aligning resources, businesses, structure, systems, and processes that are motivated by goals and objectives to fulfill its vision (Collis and Montgomery 1998, p. 9). Many organizations claim "people are our most important asset." Although this may be true, people are a necessary but not sufficient element for success. To fully maximize the human element requires organizational design aligning organizational structure, planning and control systems, human resource management, and culture to fulfill the organization's vision (Collis and Montgomery 1998, p. 135). The strategic imperative of human resource leadership is to make the vision a reality by ensuring that the structure, systems, and processes are in place for the recruitment, retention, training, and career development of the most valuable resources: people (Collis and Montgomery 1998, p. 163).

Throughout this book, we will look at various examples of how human resource leaders have viewed the trends shaping their environments—why the trends are important, what opportunities and risks they present, and how to deal with them—linking strategy and operational needs to human resource implications. These transformational human resource leaders are those who create the human resource strategy and system that results in creating organizational advantage over their competitors (Collis and Montgomery 1998, p. 7). Throughout the book, we will examine the human resource transformation as a system with the following elements:

- Culture
- Business environment
- Strategy
- Talent need
- Competencies and capabilities
- Capacity
- Human capital and innovation

As human resource leaders, we must know and do many things to be successful. We must understand and apply the fundamental knowledge of business, the specific knowledge of our own organization, and the domain knowledge of the human resource discipline. Moreover, it is critical to employ flexible and innovative thinking, applying lessons, ideas, and practices from various disciplines.

What Have Been Recent Key Trends and How Have They Changed in the Past Decade?

The Strategic Human Resource Leader (Rothwell, Prescott, and Taylor 1998b) was published based on the authors' research for "A 21st Century Vision of Strategic Human Resource Management" (Rothwell 1996) and "Seizing the Future: A Survey on Trends Affecting HR for the 21st Century" (Rothwell, Prescott, and Taylor 1998a). The trends exerting the most influence on business environment over the next ten years were expected to be the following:

- Changing technology
- Increasing globalization
- Continuing cost containment
- Increasing speed in market change
- Growing importance of knowledge capital
- Increasing rate and magnitude of change

A decade later, this chapter looks at each of the trends identified in 1998, examines how these trends have affected the greater economic environment and human resource transformation, and provides a glimpse into the future.

Changing Technology

Rapid change in technology is now expected. Harnessing it for organizational benefit is the challenge. The pace of change in information technology, communications technology, industry and product technology, revolutionary and evolutionary technology, and human know-how linking creativity, knowledge, and ability in the other technologies has a profound impact on the way we work and live (Rothwell, Prescott, and Taylor 1998b). In September 1997, Evans and Wurster (1997, pp. 71–82) correctly predicted that the new economies of information would require a transformation in organizational business and operating models, such as these:

- A new definition of economies of scale that included the ability to network vast numbers of people

- New opportunities for purely physical businesses including order fulfillment for Web businesses

- New branding opportunities for third parties to provide external credibility on performance

- Power shifts from the changed access to information previously held by the seller and therefore enabling increased comparison shopping

- A drop in customers' switching costs, thereby increasing competition at every level

- Incumbent companies stuck in the current mind-set and infrastructure and thereby losing to more nimble competitors that reframe and reshape the market

Certainly these predictions have come to fruition. One example is the growth and success of Amazon.com. Since opening in July 1995, Amazon has grown into a $10 billion Fortune 500 company. One of the most successful pioneers of online shopping, "Amazon.com, Inc. seeks to be Earth's most customer-centric company, where customers can find and discover anything they might want to buy online, and endeavors to offer its customers the lowest possible prices" (Amazon.com, Inc. 2006).

Amazon.com illustrates the use of technology, access to information, and connectivity to create a new concept to reach a global marketplace. Amazon.com boasts the following:

- A five-year growth rate of more than 25 percent, with international sales outpacing North American sales

- Product lines that include worldwide electronics, more than 35,000 health and beauty items, and over one million automotive parts and accessories for ten thousand vehicles

- Digital video downloads with access to thousands of movies, television shows, and videos through Amazon Unbox

- Web services that provide hundreds of thousands of developers with "compute" and "storage" capabilities through Amazon Elastic Compute Cloud (Amazon EC2) and Amazon Simple Storage (Amazon S3)

Today people rely on Amazon.com for quality and reliability in products and services sourced and delivered across the globe. Another example of Evans and Wurster's prediction that the new economies of information would enable transformation in organizational business and operating models is CarMax. Founded in 1993, CarMax is the largest retailer of used cars. CarMax is a Fortune 500 company and has been named to *Fortune*'s "America's Most Admired Company in Automotive Retailing" and the "100 Best Companies to Work For" (CarMax 2007).

Historically, the used car market has been characterized by locally owned dealerships, a sparcity of reliable information on vehicle price and quality, and little if any brand recognition. CarMax created a rational national market with transparency in pricing through online access to its inventory of 20,000 vehicles, access to vehicle history and maintenance records, high-quality service, and reliability. CarMax guarantees that it will not resell cars that have sustained structural damage or have been burned or flooded. It provides every car a 125-point inspection, over twelve hours of reconditioning, a thirty-day warranty, and a five-day free-return policy (www.carmax.com/dyn/companyinfo/compinfo.aspx).

CarMax' success has been fueled in large part by its customer service. Good customer service in turn has been made possible by a comprehensive career, talent management, and training policy that positions all store personnel for success (www.carmax.com). Like Amazon, CarMax has created a brand name that means open access to information, quality, and reliability. That CarMax has built a "Best Company to Work For" Fortune 500 company out of the used car industry illustrates the opportunities presented by the trend of information technology and the importance of human resources to build the talent to fulfill an organization's promise of customer service.

In addition to enabling new business models, investment in new technology and in research and development has fueled economic growth. "Between 1959 and 1995, R&D accounted for 4.5% of real GDP growth; however, it accounted for 6.7% of growth in real GDP in recent years." (*GDP*—gross domestic product—is the broadest measure of U.S. economic activity.) The importance of technological innovation is illustrated by the magnitude of the financial commitment of the private sector and the U.S. government to research and development. "The U.S. Government boasts the highest level of R&D investment in the world: $132 billion. However, unlike 40 years ago, when Federal R&D expenditures were double those of the private sector, industry R&D spending now exceeds Federal Government R&D spending." This is the highest level of discretionary outlays in thirty-seven years. "Not since 1968 and the Apollo program have we seen an investment in science of this magnitude" (Office of Science and Technology Policy, Office of the President 2006).

The impact of technology on communications, businesses, products and services, and the way that work is performed has shaped, and will continue to shape, our environment in profound ways. It fuels all of the other trends, especially globalization. Anticipating and leveraging the most important changes that technology makes to our organizations and helping to prepare the workforce are among the challenges to human resource leaders.

Increasing Globalization

"Commerce without borders, a world-wide marketplace, and international competition" were some of the ways that expert participants in

"A 21st Century Vision" (Rothwell 1996) described globalization. Enabled by communications technology, international politics, and access to new markets and labor forces, globalization has indeed continued as a significant factor in shaping the economic environment. In the 1960s, only 6 percent of the U.S. economy was exposed to international competition. In the 1980s, over 70 percent of the U.S economy was exposed ("Trends Propel New Human Resource Management Paradigm" 1996). Today, the perspective among many is that globalization opens almost everyone to competition at the same time that it opens markets.

The World Trade Organization celebrated its tenth anniversary in May 1995. Since 2001, the United States has opened international markets to 124 million consumers in twelve nations through the completion of free-trade agreements. "These agreements will create millions of new consumers for America's farmers, manufacturers, and small business owners, and deepen our friendships with countries in other parts of the world" (White House 2005). These global markets include 2.3 billion people in China and India. China has attracted more than $622 billion in total direct foreign investment and exports more than $762 billion (Gutierrez 2006). According to government statistics (White House 2006):

- U.S. exports accounted for about 25 percent of U.S. economic growth during the 1990s and supported an estimated 12 million jobs.

- Jobs in exporting plants pay wages that average up to 18 percent more than jobs in nonexporting plants.

- Approximately one out of every five factory jobs in the U.S. directly depends on trade.

- American farmers export one in three acres' worth of their crops, and exports generate nearly 25 percent of farmers' gross cash sales.

- America's dynamic high-tech sector depends on exports. In 2003, exports of advanced technology products totaled $180 billion.

The economic growth rates in countries opened for international trade are astounding. Consider the impact of the North American Free Trade Agreement (NAFTA) on members. Over the period 1993 to 2005, NAFTA policies resulted in the following:

- Growth nearing 50 percent in Canada, 48 percent in the United States, and 40 percent in Mexico

- Increases in combined trade from $300 billion to $800 billion

- The lowest unemployment rates in decades in Canada and the United States

- Single-digit inflation in Mexico (Gutierrez 2006)

In 1998, the authors of this book recommended the following to deal with globalization: Develop a global strategy; create a global identity with values, ethics, and a communication strategy; develop sensitivity to partners' concerns and to regional issues and regulations; and develop cultural awareness (Rothwell, Prescott, and Taylor 1998b). Although these recommendations are still pertinent today, the looming difference is that no organization—large or small—can avoid the impact of global competition and commerce without borders.

In today's global market, interconnected networks of consumers enabled by information technology require companies to manage brand identity and product/service offerings globally. Market and product strategies can be targeted to microsegments or a truly global audience based on sophisticated research of differences and similarities in a complex interplay of cultures, product usages, local customs, supply chains, packaging, storage, infrastructure, and marketing tools. In one of the largest and potentially most successful product launches in history, Gillette's Fusion™ razor and the complete grooming systems of shaving creams and gels were introduced with one blockbuster marketing campaign across the globe. Market research determined that attitudes toward shaving are substantially the same internationally. In contrast, Unilever demonstrates microcustomization with the reformulation of laundry detergent to the dry southern states of India, promising to reduce daily water consumption by two buckets while retaining efficacy of stain removal. Both approaches have been successful. Fusion expects to generate global annual sales of more then $1 billion (Deutsch 2005). Surf Excel experienced a 50 percent increase in sales in the target Indian states (www.unilever.com/ourbrands/homecare/Surf.asp).

Organizations have the opportunity to take advantage of global markets, economies of scale, and brand recognition. The challenge is to do the research to determine customers' buying preferences and important local differences. Human resource leaders have the obligation to analyze the implications of the global business models and align the people systems to fulfill the strategy.

To illustrate the dramatic differences in commerce without borders over the past decade, we can look at how IBM is dealing with globalization. IBM was one of the originators of the multinational business model, with each country having management, administration, manufacturing plants, and service operations. In today's environment, this model is too expensive and top-heavy. As a result, for its tech services IBM is moving to competency centers operations, which generate about $45 billion in annual revenue.

> Senior Vice President Robert W. Moffat Jr. [describes] the magnitude of this change: "For example, the change from a physical on-site installation of software onto the client's PC has dropped from $70 to 20 cents by locating a software installation factory of 200 people in Toronto that assembles packages and delivers them to machines over the Internet." IBM is taking advantage of labor arbitrage as well as scientific research capabilities to automate services. The goal is to reduce overall outsourcing costs more than 10% and provide one-third of future growth in earnings per share. Critical to the success of this transformation is ability to standardize, capture, and retrieve skills from an internal résumé bank of over 70,000 global employees. (Hamm 2006)

The IBM example illustrates one of the most important challenges presented by globalization: the need to realign the organizational structure to keep pace with the current realities of a global customer base and competitive landscape. The IBM example also illustrates the need to manage the people assets of a global workforce and to look at innovative ways to improve service while reducing costs.

Continuing Cost Containment

In the face of changing technology, rapidly changing product and service offerings, and global competition, organizations face ongoing pressures to reduce operating costs and more efficiently deploy resources.

In its 1997 *Fortune 500* issue, *Fortune* magazine noted a then remarkable phenomenon:

America's largest companies tallied up a stunning 23.3% increase in profits in 1996—an extraordinary performance in the sixth year of a recovery. Not only did earnings sprint ahead in 1996: they grew faster than revenues, which increased 8.3%. This uncommonly—and ultimately unsustainable—phenomenon has been occurring for four straight years. That means corporate America, hell-bent on controlling costs, is still finding new ways to squeeze more profit from each dollar of sales. (Henkoff 1997, p. 193)

Cost containment efforts included reducing waste and inefficiency, increasing productivity, lowering breakeven points, offsetting labor costs with increased technology, and using nontraditional salary and expense reductions. In 1998, common approaches to containing costs included restructuring the organization to reduce head count (downsizing), forming joint ventures and outsourcing relationships, substituting technology for people, revaluing the supply chain, refinancing capital structure, and reducing staff functions. The need for cost containment has translated in many cases to an increase in outsourcing, offshoring, and other business models that allow for overall lower cost, such as taking advantage of labor arbitrage or business models that are variable "pay by the drink" (Rothwell 1996).

Over the past decade, the push to capture cost advantage has continued to propel the global economy through the desire to take advantage of lower-cost wages in developing countries. Growth rates in China and India were primary contributors to the record 4.25 percent growth of the global economy in 2006 (McGirt 2006, p. 194). "The China price" generally refers to a price 30 percent to 50 percent less than in the United States. "What is stunning about China is that for the first time we have a huge, poor country that can compete both with very low wages and in high tech," says Harvard University economist Richard B. Freeman (Engardio, Roberts, and Bremner 2004). India's growth has proceeded at more than 8 percent over the past five years, and the government expects it to continue at 9 percent through 2012. Firms such as Infosys and Tata Steel have become globally successful ("India on Fire" 2007).

In a March 2006 *McKinsey Quarterly* survey, executives from all industries except banking and financial services ranked "more low cost competitors" first or second as the most important "single factor that contributes most to the increasing competitive intensity in your indus-try today" ("Global Survey of Business Executives" 2006). The contin-ued focus on cost containment is evidenced by organizations' efforts in supply chain and logistics management, implementation of Six Sigma and lean manufacturing initiatives, growth in outsourcing, and radical shifts in compensation and benefits such as consumer-driven health care and the elimination of pension plans. In fact, the *SHRM Workplace Forecast for 2006–2007* placed the rising cost of health care and the resulting negative impact on U.S. competitiveness as the number one trend affecting the workplace and human resources (Society for Human Resource Management 2006, p. 2).

A look at General Motors emphasizes the importance of cost reduc-tions to stay competitive. On November 11, 2006, Tony Clarke, presi-dent of General Motors, stated, "I recognize that the GM that I grew up in no longer exists. I have no romantic notions of returning to the good old days. We're a much different company today, and we're not done with our transformation." Further, Clarke said that the company must make dramatic changes to the overall cost structure to reduce costs by 25 percent and that it must increase sales (Clarke 2006).

GM's woes exemplify the rising concern about health care costs. GM's spends $1,525 in health expenditures for each car it builds. This is more than the cost of the steel in each car. The impact on GM's compet-itiveness is illustrated by declining market share. In 1962, GM had a 50 percent share of the American car market. Today that share is 25 percent (Will 2005, p. B7).

In the first quarter of 2007, Toyota celebrated its fiftieth anniversary in the United States by selling more cars than General Motors. Many credit the Toyota Production System, the pioneer of lean manufactur-ing, for the low cost and high quality that have fueled Toyota's popular-ity (Jones 2007). The Toyota Camry has earned the title of the best-sell-ing passenger car in America for nearly a decade. The Toyota Corolla, introduced in 1968, has become the world's best-selling car with over 27 million sold in more than 140 countries. By 2010, Toyota will build 2.2 million cars and 1.45 million engines in fifteen plants in the United States (Toyota Motor Corporation 2007).

Concerns about reducing costs to remain competitive force human resource leaders to be vigilant to ensure that staffing models use the lowest-cost labor possible, to reduce spending on compensation and benefits packages, to evaluate outsourcing and offshoring, and to automate jobs to reduce labor. Many successful human resource departments are also embracing the process improvement and change management techniques of lean manufacturing and Six Sigma to improve the quality of their services.

Increasing Speed in Market Change

Since 1998, speed in market change has influenced the environment as both a cause and an effect of market volatility. Influenced by increases in technology and available information, especially in the service sector, the market changes rapidly, and the importance of speed in reacting to market changes has been and will continue to be one of the significant trends affecting business organizations. Virtual organizations, fluidity in access to resources through alliances and joint ventures, and the ease of reaching global customers through the Internet have all continued to feed the volatility of markets, shorten product life cycles, and ease the entry of new players (Rothwell, Prescott, and Taylor 1998a). Some impacts of the speed of market change include destabilization of industries, increased customer expectation for new products and services, and the need for market information.

In 2006, 24 percent of those surveyed in the *McKinsey* Global Survey of Business Executives said that the "single factor that contributes to increased competition is innovation in products, services, and business models" ("Global Survey of Business Executives" 2006).

An organization can deal with speed in market change using the following strategies (Rothwell, Prescott, and Taylor 1998b, p. 153):

- Lead the market.
- Build an organization that can respond quickly to change by being flexible, integrated, and innovative.
- Develop business strategies that serve to balance people, process, and technology.
- Know how to build a strategic organization.
- Apply strategic thinking.

- Recognize that organizational culture plays a part in the change process.

- Develop and implement a new product strategy.

The ability to innovate and launch fresh, relevant products and services faster and with more sustainability than the competition is critical to survival. Often, new product strategy is an extension of current offerings to existing, similar, or adjacent customers. In the face of such rapidly changing markets, organizations are also faced with the need to create innovative new businesses that address new solutions, new markets, and new technologies. Often, experienced leaders reject promising new opportunities because "they are too different" and "that is not the way we do it here." Successful managers are made uneasy by the typical lack of supporting market data, fear of cannibalization, and pronounced differences inherent in emerging business models. The entrepreneurial mind-set required for business start-up is diametrically opposed to that of maximizing the efficiency of an ongoing concern. Companies that are successful at new business start-up learn to exploit the ambiguous environment by incorporating experimentation, identifying critical success criteria, closely observing and learning from real customers interacting with the product, and quickly moving to prototype. These companies are also willing to learn, revise, reframe, and if needed abandon ideas. Also critical is the ability to exploit the company's existing strengths and management talent (Garvin and Levesque 2006).

Innovation in all aspects of the organization contributes to increasing speed in dealing with market change. A major contributor is the use of flexible teaming arrangements like joint ventures, partnerships, consultancies, and contract workers. By drawing upon others' competencies and reducing the start-up time, these arrangements accelerate the speed an organization can achieve in going from concept to market with a new product or service. Increasing in popularity are techniques such as design for manufacturability and concurrent engineering, which are proven to reduce costs and time to market by as much as 50 percent. Cross-functional product development teams—comprising marketing, manufacturing, testing, supply chain, regulatory, packaging, and service—work together to ensure that operational processes and constraints are built into the design process. By making decisions in the design phase about use of existing manufacturing processes, standard parts, and experienced suppliers, organizations can reduce costs, increase speed to market, and enhance customer satisfaction (Anderson 2007).

Human resource leaders play an important role in creating a culture that values speed to market and innovation by working closely with business leaders in identifying opportunities for experimentation with organization design, talent management, and succession planning to provide entrepreneurial experiences and learning that often includes the extended enterprise. Tom Kelley, general manager of IDEO and author of the best-selling *Art of Innovation,* discusses the importance of innovation as a pivotal part of a company's culture: "Sure, a great product can be one important element in the formula for business success, but companies who want to succeed in today's competitive environment need much more. They need innovation at every point of the compass, in all aspects of the business and among every team member." This requires creating a culture of positive change that is rich in creativity. "And companies that want to succeed at innovation will need new insights. New viewpoints. And new roles" (Kelley and Littman 2005, p. 3).

New insights, new roles, and new viewpoints—through what people know and how they use that knowledge—lead to the next trend and to the essence of the human resource leader's mandate.

Growing Importance of Knowledge Capital

In 1997 Peter Drucker (p. 20) eloquently captured the essence of the growing importance of knowledge capital:

> Economic growth can no longer come either from putting more people to work—that is, from more resource input, as much of it has come in the past—or from an increase in consumers' demands. It can come only from a very sharp and continuing increase in the productivity of the one resource in which the developed countries still have a competitive edge (and one which they are likely to maintain for a few more decades): knowledge work and knowledge workers.

Economic growth is driven by the skillful application of human talent and creativity to realize quantum breakthroughs in innovation, productivity, product and service quality, and customer satisfaction (Rothwell, Prescott, and Taylor 1998b). *Knowledge capital* is defined as the collective economic value of the organization's workforce, including the institutional memory, the current talent pool, and creativity. As the importance of knowledge increases and the ability to capture, transmit, and distribute it electronically instantaneously across the globe increases, the more temporal the knowledge becomes, resulting in rapid changes to products, services, and even entire markets. At the same time, the knowledge and expertise that are inherently possessed by individuals will become increasingly more important and mobile, resulting in the changing nature of organizations and employee relationships. As a result, managing the knowledge resources of an enterprise, including that of suppliers, contractors, consultants, and partners, will become the most important harbinger of success (Drucker et al. 1997, pp. 22–24).

The focus on knowledge capital has been increasing. Recommendations for managing with the growing importance of knowledge capital include the following (Rothwell, Prescott, and Taylor 1998b, pp. 191–195):

- Prepare for the realities and need to educate the workforce.
- Invest in people as a competitive asset.
- Look at long-term plans for the workplace.
- Support ways to deploy knowledge assets.
- Revisit matrix management.
- Develop teams.
- Develop rewards systems for knowledge sharing.
- Create strategies to develop knowledge capital in succession planning.

One of the biggest challenges is searching out and capturing what is most valuable to an organization: the contextual, applied knowledge gained from experience. Despite the plethora of knowledge management tools and best efforts to capture, categorize, and distribute knowledge, the transfer and practical application of tacit knowledge remains elusive. Exemplar organizations create a system-wide multifaceted approach.

At the time that *The Strategic Human Resource Leader* was written in 1998, organizations aspired to become "learning organizations." British Petroleum (BP), led until May 2007 by Lord John Browne, exemplified that descriptor, creating knowledge architectures, managing knowledge assets as a priority, and creating communities of practice throughout its global employee base, suppliers, partners, and customers (Rothwell, Prescott, and Taylor 1998b, pp. 186–189). BP pioneered an approach to knowledge management that learns and codifies knowledge before, during, and after an event or project. Three simple but powerful processes, the Peer Assist, the After Action Review, and the Retrospect, draw expertise from across the enterprise, immediately improve the performance of the project at hand, and create a body of knowledge that can be leveraged in the future. Among the most important keys to BP's success in applying knowledge management are participation, sharing, and an attitude that change is expected, valued, and rewarded.

Six Sigma is commonly thought of as a manufacturing-based statistical approach to save costs and eliminate defects. Many companies have implemented it with mediocre results. However, firms such as General Electric, Honeywell, Motorola, Texas Instruments, Raytheon, and SAIC have been wildly successful, often achieving financial results in the billions. The most successful firms combine lean manufacturing and Six Sigma with knowledge management and change leadership to institutionalize an approach that creates a culture of using data-driven decision making and process improvement. Perhaps the longest-lasting and hardest-to-quantify result is that these firms create networks of people with common processes, decision tools, group facilitation protocols, language, and responsibility to make changes in the operation to improve performance and customer satisfaction. All successful firms have taken the approach well beyond that of an initiative and are characterized by demonstrably supportive leadership, in-depth and enterprise-wide communication and training, the quantification and expectation of results, and supportive infrastructure to enable the capture of knowledge.

Over the past decade, the importance of valuing what people know has given rise to the imperatives for human capital strategy planning and comprehensive talent management. Many organizations are taking a holistic view toward planning and educating their extended enterprise, including suppliers, customers, and partners. This is especially important given the prevalence of nontraditional corporate structures and the demographic trends that include huge numbers of impending retirees. "Human capital strategic planning is looking at your current workforce or your current inventory, looking ahead at what your future requirements are and where you need to go," according to Sue Greemore, executive director of Defense Contract Management Agency (DCMA) Human Resources. "The difference between what you have and what you need is then your gap. The Human Capital Strategic Plan defines what strategies or actions you need to take to close the gap. It really sets your transformation roadmap for your transformation management" (Greemore 2005, p. 1).

Increasing Rate and Magnitude of Change

Change is driven by the need for survival of the organization. Technology, globalization, political pressures, demographic shifts, change in markets, and consumer needs—all result in the need for organizations to redefine themselves in order to survive. Over the past decade, the pace of change has accelerated, and it will continue to do so. Although the acceleration of change is not surprising, there has been a marked shift in the ways in which organizations change.

During the 1990s the prevailing wisdom and basis of many change management consultancies was a top-down, leader-driven, structured change process that included the requisite executive sponsorship; identification of the "burning platform" of underlying causes; identification of negative impacts of the status quo and positive outcomes of the change effort; and carrying on of communication blitzes, training, and project teams to create buy-in. Many of these efforts were successful and were reflective of the business environment at the time. Many others based on traditional planning "collapse[d] under the weight of their own intensity" as they were not designed for successful execution (Hirshhorn 2002, p. 98).

Today, organizations are using a much more viral method of change that takes advantage of existing social networks and the connectivity of instant communications. Firms that successfully combine Six Sigma, knowledge management, and change management are drawing on this viral change model—connected networks powered by common tools with the mandate to solve problems. Employees get excited, get involved, and make a difference quickly.

The Campaign Approach to Change created by the Center for Applied Research (CFAR) illustrates an approach that gets employees' attention and help. This approach is especially effective in organizations with a diffuse base of authority. Combining metaphors from politics, marketing and advertising, and the military, the Campaign Approach has the following key elements (Center for Applied Research 1999):

- **Listen in on the institution:** Spend time in the field observing and talking to people. See firsthand examples of the desired future "found pilots" in nascent practice and exploit their success to generate more change.

- **Develop a strategic theme:** Frame a theme to energize people and give direction. Iterate on the theme and create an emotional hook based on what people are saying.

- **Sweep people in:** Give opportunities to emerging leaders to act. Be broadly inclusive.

- **Create the infrastructure:** Use a project team that can "drive strategy, orchestrate volunteers" and "stay on top of breaking events." Be prepared to capture and hold people's time and attention by building momentum and results for them personally.

Drawing on these techniques can help human resource leaders to better perform one of their most critical roles, that of change agent. The ability to lead a successful change initiative is essential to the role of the human resource leader. Human resource leaders are at the center of creating change in the enterprise and in their own departments. The role includes acting as a strategic partner, listener, adviser, and coach to the executive and leadership team, creating governance and communication, and working with employees in all facets of change.

How Do Trends Relate to HR Transformation?

Much has been written about the role of human resources and the competencies of human resource professionals, and many books have been written by and for human resource professionals. Although most of the research acknowledges that the ultimate goal of human resource management is to facilitate the ultimate success of the primary organization, the treatment is often cursory. To be successful, the human resource organization must focus on creating a human capital system that can deal with the trends that affect the operating environment of an organization in such a way as to create success as defined by the specific goals of that organization. Understanding the existing and emerging influences and creating a human capital system must be the primary focus of the human resource function.

Human resource departments are being asked to "recharter," or come up with a new mission, new goals, and new objectives to support business efforts. Most often this HR transformation is occurring as a result of transformation in major organizations. Many of the trends that we discuss are a driving force for transformation in the organizational strategy and operations. These trends affect the competitive environment, business conditions, and even world politics. We refer to these as changes in the workplace. Other trends affect the way in which our organizations are made up or how demographics affect and change the composition of the workforce. Most of the trends are so interrelated as to be both the causes and the effects of the other trends. In fact, it is difficult, if not almost impossible, to completely isolate a specific trend to create a one-to-one relationship between an organizational impact and a trend.

Taking into account business perspective and general management thinking is vital to HR transformation. At times, human resource professionals give a nod to the business issues, then quickly proceed to talk about their own issues in a language using terms that are uniquely technical in HR. These discussions are often not really understood or cared about by managers focused on serving customers, running operations, and generating profits. Finally, and perhaps most important, success is not gained by simply following a few simple steps with a superficial look at the business case. Although we present tools, processes, and even templates, these are only implements in the process. Successful organizational and human resource transformation will be brought about only by a deep understanding of the complex organizational environment and its challenges, a real knowledge of what is needed operationally, and critical thinking and influencing skills.

How Do Different Stakeholder Groups Regard HR, and Why Are Their Evaluations Important?

In 1973, about 25 percent of American workers belonged to unions, and powerful unions affected politics and most employers. This number began to drop in the 1980s, and today less than 12 percent of the U.S. workforce belongs to unions. This decline is partially attributable to the decline in the manufacturing sector and the globalization of corporations. During the economic downturn in the late 1970s and early 1980s, the contentious relationships and union demands contributed to the high cost and decreased competitiveness of many plants and entire companies in the heavy manufacturing sectors of steel, chemicals, autos, and textiles. These problems required companies to rethink how they did business and how they related to unions; hence, how they used human resources.

In a speech on December 7, 2006, Troy Clarke, president of GM North America, illustrated the impact of human resource strategy and action on their business in reaching a historic agreement with the United Auto Workers (UAW) to create savings of $1 billion in health care costs and to manage an attrition plan. "I really do have to give credit to the UAW for their commitment to helping General Motors address this tough issue. The agreement was negotiated during the middle of an existing contract, at a time when there really was no obligation to discuss these challenges. Yet, everyone was willing to roll up their sleeves and work through a very difficult situation." Clarke continued, "Overall, I'm really proud of how our plants have managed the attrition plan. Our safety and quality remains excellent—we haven't missed a beat. That's thanks to a lot of hard work, a focus on training, and the consistency provided by our global manufacturing system. It's also thanks to some very good union-management relationships" (Clarke 2006).

The General Motors case is a profound illustration of the constituents of human resources and the roles of HR and managers. As an exercise for setting the context of an HR transformation, ask yourself the following questions about GM:

- Who are the constituents and what are their primary interests?
- What are the opinions of the executive level, the managerial levels, the union representatives, and the front-line employees?
- What is the purpose of transformation?
- What is the correct vertical and horizontal fit of HR?

Next, imagine a similar headline for your organization on a pressing strategic constraint. As a final question, how well is your human resource group serving each of the groups?

To think about the power of HR transformation in the face of the ever-changing environment, read the Transformation in Action example "Explosive Growth and Global Talent Management."

TRANSFORMATION IN ACTION

Explosive Growth and Global Talent Management

We spoke with Judy, executive vice president of Human Resources for a leading global services firm, to discuss how the trends have affected her organization over the past ten years and what she anticipated to be the biggest impacts on the future of the business. Her responses to our questions epitomize the dynamic nature of organization and human resource transformation over the past decade and into the future.

One of the key highlights of the past ten years, Judy explained, is that the size of the company has more than doubled. Many do not realize that when the CEO sets a goal of 10 percent annual growth, it is a mandate to double the size of the company. While an organization can typically assimilate 10 percent growth in the next year, the cumulative result of 10 percent year after year is quite different. An organization twice as large as it was formerly cannot and should not operate in the same way today as it did then. HR needs to be proactive in dealing with the implications of change, which will include new customers, new markets, new regions, new products and services, and the requisite organizational and talent development challenges.

For many industries, the projected growth rates in the United States are limited. To achieve our future growth goals, we are expanding into new international markets and changing the way we go to market. As we grow into a truly global company, leveraging innovation and data-driven decision making across the enterprise to make clients more successful, creating a global brand image and a global talent management system becomes increasingly important.

Historically, each business unit sold independently. Today, clients demand integrated solutions that require client account teams to be a global resource, integrating elements from across the enterprise. We are increasingly working with partners with strong brand identity to integrate them into client solutions. Many of the client issues are the same in every country. To ensure that innovative ideas are shared across the globe, the company restructured from multiple business units into four sectors reporting to four presidents. These sectors share talent and initiatives worldwide. Within the past year, there were ten global management movements. The goal is to move process and structure integration through talent management. While the company can leverage innovation and best practices, it cannot simply dictate rules and standard processes from corporate headquarters. Each account must be handled differently to maximize satisfaction and financial return, emphasizing the importance of integrated talent management.

Global labor issues will become increasingly challenging as human resources must deal globally with compliance, health, welfare, and pension issues while accommodating the differences in labor laws and regulations in each of its countries. Recently, the company was picketed at a client site in the United States because of a foreign labor dispute. Years ago, each business unit could afford to negotiate separately with labor unions. Today, the company has a centralized labor and employment group to negotiate on behalf of the company as a whole.

The global talent management process is geared to hiring the right people and giving them the right start and retention. When multiple business units managed talent independently, there were no efficiencies and no quality control. At one point, the company worked with more than fifty executive search firms. Today, a newly established position, the director of executive recruiting, coordinates the efforts of ten executive search firms and a leading leadership assessment firm. Each executive candidate is assessed for cultural fit. The executive recruiting firms and the leadership assessment firm go through an annual orientation to get updated on the company's strategic and market plans. The result is a dramatic increase in talent quality and a decrease in recruiting costs.

Because of the significant amount of responsibility and travel that a manager assumes immediately, as well as historical difficulty in retaining new management talent, the company has implemented a one-year on-boarding process. This includes a new team assimilation and assignment to an executive coach from the leadership assessment firm, which conducts periodic interviews with the new managers' teams, leaders, and peers to assess the assimilation; offers coaching on the opportunities and challenges identified; and leads interventions if needed. The on-boarding process also includes the assignment of an internal mentor responsible for a defined process that includes meeting with executives, sharing information on how to get things done, and providing check-points on progress.

While we employ hundreds of thousand people around the world, the top three hundred leaders create the future of our business. They set the strategy and the agenda for growth. Within the past year, the company completely redesigned the Executive Leadership Development program. The new program aligns the business and market strategy with the newly developed leadership competency model; ensures cross-business collaboration and networking; provides an enterprise-wide coaching network to drive consistency, behavior, and feedback; and offers exposure to global thought leaders and company executives.

The services company case sets the context for the Human Resource Transformation Roadmap. Figure 2-1 outlines a road map to assess your organization for Human Resource Transformation. The critical success factor in leading a transformation is to look at the changes required to prepare for the future of the organization. While the future is unknown, we can begin to identify some of the transformational activities that we should undertake today by studying the trends affecting our environment, as well as the stated organizational strategic direction and business capabilities needed to fulfill these ambitions. Then we envision the desired future state of our business and human resources, characterize the gap between the current and the future state, and determine from that gap the priorities for action today and in the future. The speed and

> degree of change required are determined by the size of the gap and the magnitude and velocity of future environmental and business change.

The essence of human resource transformation is the ability to translate the ever-changing competitive environment and the organizational strategies into systems and processes that align the energies and knowledge of people with the common organizational vision. It is also having the perspective and the willingness to question the status quo and to change.

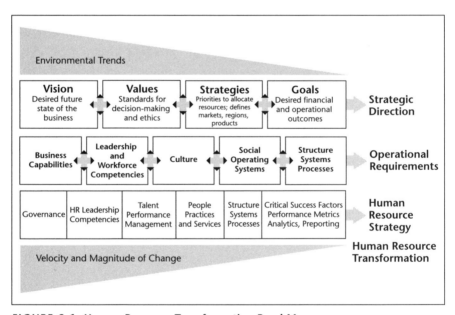

FIGURE 2-1. Human Resource Transformation Road Map

Part Two

Focusing on Future Trends

Future Trends
in the Workplace

This chapter explores the future trends in the workplace, using these questions:

- What are the key future workplace trends?
- What themes underlie the trends?
- What causes the trends?
- What are the likely impacts of the trends?
- How should the impacts of the trends be managed?
- What do the trends mean for HR transformation?

What Are the Key Future Workplace Trends?

Like tributaries flowing into a river, many of the recent trends combine to create even more powerful forces shaping the next decade and beyond. To examine the future workplace trends, the authors have had conversations with numerous executives and human resource leaders, performed a broad literature search, and studied recent surveys. The resulting perspectives represent the views of more than five thousand executives and human resource leaders from around the world who articulated the threats and opportunities to sustaining profitable global growth and the resulting implications for human resources. The three overarching future workplace trends are these:

- Globalization and the resulting impact on regions, markets, and talent

- Technology and shifts in sectors changing the type of work needed and how that work is done

- A change in the nature of organizations and employee relationships

What Themes Underlie the Trends?

From the requirement to deal with all of these trends simultaneously and the complexity of operating in a global environment, we are seeing emerging leadership and talent management requirements that are pertinent to large multinational corporations, governments, and nonprofits, as well as to small, midsize, and emerging organizations. The authors believe that these issues will provide the context for future human resource imperatives and transformation over the next decade.

Globalization

Globalization presents "a powerful and unstoppable force" (Pricewater-houseCoopers 2007, p. 4). To remain competitive, executives must lead their companies to profitable growth in new markets with new technologies and products. The most important challenges and opportunities presented by the changing environment include the following:

- Profound shifts in the centers of economic power

- Explosion of new consumers

- New global industry and organizational structures

Although the United States will continue to provide the largest share of absolute economic growth in the next two decades, growth in developing regions will profoundly change the power base of economic activity. Today Asia makes up about 13 percent and Western Europe 30 percent of world GDP. Over the next two decades, the two shares will converge (Davis and Stephenson 2006, p. 1). By 2050, the E7 (the seven economies consisting of Brazil, Russia, India, and China combined with the emerging economies of Indonesia, Mexico, and Turkey) will outstrip the current G7 (the United States, Japan, Germany, the United Kingdom, France, Italy, and Canada) (PricewaterhouseCoopers 2007, p. 7).

The economic growth in these regions will create vast new markets with new consumers. Over the next decade, almost a billion new consumers will emerge with income levels that exceed $5,000 a year, allowing them to make expenditures on discretionary goods. By 2015, the spending power of consumers in developing economies is expected to more than double, to $9 trillion, roughly equivalent to that of Western Europe (Davis and Stephenson 2006, p. 2). Early investment is paying off for global firms such as General Motors, Motorola, and Proctor and Gamble that have penetrated the Chinese market, which has a middle-class that is expected to number about 200 million people by 2010 (Engardio, Roberts, and Bremner 2004).

The changing needs among ethnic groups and demographic cohorts will alter the demand for products and services. The one million immigrants that enter the United States annually will result in one in four in the population being Asian or Hispanic by 2030 (Frey 1999). Millennials, more than 76 million strong, already outnumbering baby boomers, and representing a cross-cultural, global phenomenon, are beginning the full force of their adolescent and adult spending years. The boomers, as they edge toward retirement and a potentially long old age, will continue to shape markets for products and services, especially health care, leisure, and financial services (Howe and Strauss 2000). These consumer segments present opportunities for innovation in offerings of products and services as well as challenges in dealing with social responsibility in issues of access to health care and protection of the environment.

New structures of global organizations and industries are emerging. The largest corporations are growing both organically and through acquisitions, using their economies of scale to slowly transition from being multinational to being more nearly global in structure. At the same time, smaller, more innovative, and more agile companies continue to enter the competitive field. Organizations are increasingly working in collaboration with partners to combine core competencies, relationships, and market access in unique ways (Davis and Stephenson 2006, p. 3). Volatility in structures of organizations and industries creates a need for responsiveness and agility among both employees and human resource leaders.

Technology

Rapid advancements in technology will continue to change the way work is performed and where it is performed in two fundamental ways:

- Technological connectivity
- Changing economics of knowledge

Globally connected communications technology will change the way people work, play, and socialize. The ability to capture, store, manipulate, and transmit information provides opportunity for more scientific and analytical decision making and operations. Merging technologies will result in unprecedented opportunities for solving problems, for example through the use of laser technology in health care and biotechnology. Global connectivity will remove the constraint of place in which work is performed (Davis and Stephenson 2006, p. 2). Connectivity also changes the communication and power structure of organizations to less-hierarchical and more-networked forms. Organizations are just beginning to exploit the possibilities.

The changing economics of knowledge remove traditional barriers to entry for knowledge-based businesses. Technology is providing access to information, and investment in research and development is producing new knowledge at unprecedented rates. The ability to collaborate virtually and develop across communities will change the way that organizations capture knowledge. New technology tools are emerging to capture and facilitate virtual collaboration. Creating business protocols that encourage this collaboration while protecting the security of information and intellectual property in a virtual global environment poses significant challenges, especially given vast differences in regulatory environments.

The level of new knowledge creation also creates the need for deeper and more specialized expertise. In this environment, the tacit knowledge of subject matter experts becomes increasingly valuable and more difficult to institutionalize. Organizations become more vulnerable to loss of key subject matter expertise.

Vast quantities of information will increasingly be available for analysis and insight into markets, customers, competitors, operational performance, and workforce performance, resulting in the need for data-driven decision making. Leaders will be challenged to be savvier using quantitative analysis to drive business decisions tools while not being overwhelmed by the sheer volume of available data. The availability of statistical analysis tools and Six Sigma initiatives can push problem-solving ability into lower levels of the organization.

Changing Employment Relationships

The increasing need for rapid organizational change to react quickly to new markets and competitors leads to volatility in organizational structure and a shift in employment relationships. With retirement and benefits costs equaling on average 42 percent of payroll costs, organizations carefully scrutinize the need for full-time salaried workers. Availability of communications technology and virtual connectivity, along with changing requirements and the erosion of the old employment contract of job security in exchange for loyalty, has resulted in a dramatic increase in the number of free agents. The number of one-person businesses is growing by 4–5 percent a year. The average length of tenure is decreasing: The average length of time American males aged fifty-five to sixty-four have been with their employers declined from 15.3 years in 1983 to 10.2 years in 2000. Forty percent of employees have expressed an interest in working somewhere new, and 40 percent of midlevel managers retain relationships with recruiters ("Masters of the Universe" 2006).

The nature of work is also changing. Automation and information technology are changing both the types of jobs available and their nature—fewer hands-on jobs and more virtual automated transactions. This technology also creates the virtual worker who is connected via cell phone and computer in the telecommuting mobile office that can be almost anywhere. Many corporations have dramatically reduced layers of supervision and continue to restructure. Formal and restrictive jobs and work rules are diminishing, having been replaced by requirements for employees to adapt to changing demands of new strategies, products, and service offerings (O'Toole and Lawler 2006, pp. 40–55).

Ours has been dubbed the "Anxiety Economy" to illustrate the way many Americans are feeling about today's business environment. Although rates of GDP growth, unemployment, and inflation, productivity gains, and corporate profits are all positive, anxiety persists over slow wage growth and lack of job security. China and India make up 40 percent of the global labor force and through technology are potentially poised to take over "tradable services"—jobs that do not need to be done in person (Regnier 2007, p. 96).

Although the number of jobs moving offshore is growing, the number of total jobs lost to date is less than the number of jobs lost and added to the U.S. economy in a two-week period. According to University of Chicago labor economist Steven Davis, the perception of job loss in the United States may seem more pronounced than it is in reality because it affects two groups. First, job security has declined for college-educated men, a group that historically had been relatively insulated from economic volatility. Second, the stability of employment of publicly traded corporations has decreased. Although these corporations employ only one-third of all workers, they receive the most attention from the news media and investors (Regnier 2007, p. 97). In fact, less than 20 percent of Americans work for Fortune 1000 companies, which are America's largest publicly held corporations and the ones most likely to be global. Small businesses account for approximately 50 percent of American jobs and create 75 percent of new ones. Another 19 percent work for government agencies, and 8 percent work for nonprofit organizations (O'Toole and Lawler 2006, p. 22).

What Causes the Trends?

Interconnected forces cause dramatic shifts in the workplace and in the ways in which we do business. A vast majority of surveyed executives, 85 percent, describe their company's business environment as more competitive than it was five years ago. The primary drivers of the accelerating pace of change are innovation in products, services, and business models; rate of technology change; the free flow of information; and the elements of globalization—access to capital, labor, and markets through reduced trade barriers ("An Executive Take on the Top Business Trends" 2006, pp. 1–2).

In the face of accelerating global competitive pressures, executives remain generally positive about the future and see opportunity for profitable growth. Table 3-1 outlines how executives rank their degree of concern about potential threats to their businesses.

As leaders strategize ways to exploit the opportunities and mitigate risk in a volatile environment, emphasis will be on the ability to quickly mobilize resources with organizational structure, business processes, virtual relationships, and global talent. Intertwining cause and effect and the changing nature of organizational and industrial structure, combined with the changing nature of employment relationships, results in a vastly different workplace than even a decade ago. Looking into the future, the authors envision the structure of organizations and industries and employment relationships to be increasingly varied and flexible, with both opportunities and risks.

TABLE 3-1			
CEOs' and Executives' Concerns About Potential Business Threats			
Threat	% extremely concerned	% somewhat concerned	% not very concerned	% not at all concerned
---	---	---	---	---
Over-regulation	40	33	21	6
Availability of key skills	39	33	21	6
Low-cost competition	34	32	23	11
Energy prices	29	33	26	12
Commodity prices	23	35	28	14
Downturn in major economies	22	35	34	8

Source: Adapted from PricewaterhouseCoopers, Tenth Annual Global CEO Survey, 2007; http://www.pwc.com/ceosurvey.

What Are the Likely Impacts of the Trends?

For the first time, executives are demonstrating a pronounced shift in focus away from viewing the flow of financial capital as the primary driver of global growth. The abilities to attract talent, harness knowledge into intellectual property, and create a culture of innovation and collaboration across an extended network of stakeholders are the primary drivers of future global success. Conversely, the inability to build this culture of talent may be the most important barrier to growth. More than 70 percent of executives view the lack of critical skills and talent as a potential business threat. Executives are increasingly focused on developing a global talent base and leadership perspectives to create global, sustainable, and profitable growth (PricewaterhouseCoopers 2007, p. 1).

In their simplest form, the trends force leaders to envision how the work can best get done and by whom. Gone is the requirement for much of the work to be done "in place." As a result, organizations can determine where the best skills are for the best value—even if they are from outside of the firm. Connectivity, changing demographics, and cost pressures are resulting in a new look at human capital and organizational structure and what provides the best value in a holistic approach across the entire constellation of an organization's relationships.

How Should the Impacts of the Trends Be Managed?

Increasingly complex organizational structures, access to global markets and talent, and the need to manage across geographic and organizational borders will require different leadership perspectives. Tomorrow's leaders will need to be comfortable with collaborative approaches to working across the extended enterprise, with sophisticated decision-making tools, and with sensitivity to social responsibility and environmental sustainability. Executives articulate the importance of developing leaders with a global perspective and the willingness to invest in programs to develop that perspective.

As the availability of knowledge and the technology to capture and analyze this information increases, the ability to attract, develop, and retain the necessary skills sets will increase. Organizations will need to compete globally for the best and brightest talent. Critical technical and managerial expertise is not easily replicated, as it is the result of cycles of on-the-job application and tacit knowledge. The quest to accelerate the readiness of those in areas of scarce expertise is mounting, exacerbated by the degree of integrative knowledge required by today's interconnecting technologies and complex organizations. Organizations that are able to develop talent across the extended enterprise and create both the skills sets and global values will be the most successful.

For example, one of the scarcest resources in the aerospace and defense industry is that of systems engineers. To be a successful systems engineer requires the ability to conceptualize a solution to a complex problem, link various engineering and other technical disciplines together from a systems design and team collaboration standpoint, and manage the business and technical aspects of a program from concept through design, development, and delivery. Traditionally, this interdisciplinary technical and business-minded approach has not been taught in universities. Many in the industry believe that the ability to develop this scarce resource will be a primary factor in future growth.

The new employment relationship has advantages and disadvantages on both sides of the equation. From the vantage point of the organization, it is in a competitive and global market for talent. Human resource leaders need to recognize and address the fact that the stakes are higher; at the same time, the potential rewards are higher in terms of using the right people at the right time for the right price. Human resource leaders should also recognize that the changing employee relationship transfers some risks that have been borne by large corporations to the employee. The transfer of risk to the employee takes on the following dimensions:

- Nineteen percent of today's workers have a traditional pension plan, a drop from 62 percent twenty years ago.

- The majority of employer-sponsored plans are 401(k)-type plans.

- Forty-seven million Americans, of whom 22 million have full-time jobs, do not have health insurance. (Regnier 2007, p. 96)

Many organizations are helping employees to better manage their risk-return trade-offs; 401(k) plans, consumer-driven health care, and company-sponsored training both inside and outside of the firm are all a part of that equation. Other organizations are developing new products, services, and tools to educate and serve these employees. For example, Fidelity offers a series of educational products and tools on its Web site, www.401k.com, and many of the health insurers and benefit providers believe that education is now a part of their competitive differentiator. As human resource leaders, we should be aware of our role in selecting providers and offering educational programs to help our employees make better decisions on their health, benefits, and investments.

It is tempting to look at and react to each of these trends, risks, and changes individually; the outcome would be frustration at best and chaos at worst. Instead, the authors propose taking an integrated view of linking human capital strategy to organizational strategy. The U.S. Navy has what is arguably one of the most complex staffing systems, comprising active duty military, government workers, defense contractors, and freelancers, all within the constraints of the oversight of the U.S. government defense and procurement regulations. An example from this perhaps surprising source illustrates taking advantage of the trends and creating a human capital planning system to fulfill mission, increase capability, reduce costs, and create alignment.

In a for-profit corporation, success or value creation is measured by the return of wealth to the corporation's shareholders. In a government or not-for-profit organization, success is measured by how effectively the organization fulfills its stated mission to safeguard public welfare within budget constraints. In all types of organizations, the goal to maximize the return on the resources invested is appropriate. Although successful government agencies demonstrate many of the same critical success factors as successful corporations, they face unique challenges. Often leaders are appointed on the basis of their political prowess or technical expertise and have only a short tenure. All aspects of the agency's operations, people, and outcomes are examined and reported on by the general public, elected officials, and the news media, combined with the myriad constituents and stakeholders, resulting in overwhelming complexity and resistance to change (Ostroff 2006, p. 142). With mind-numbing constraints and complexities, all of the changing environmental dynamics, and the gravity of consequences of mission failure, change efforts are even more remarkable and full of insights.

Human resource leaders in any organization can use the following key principles:

- **Improve performance against mission:** Clarify the overarching objective and vision. Rally employees and leaders around a clear and simple definition. Always analyze how actions will contribute to the mission.

- **Win over stakeholders:** Understand who all of the stakeholders are internally and externally and how groups of them will resist and benefit. Be creative and even dramatic in demonstrating and winning them over. Simultaneously focus on the most critical to the campaign's success, and stretch to be sure to include less obvious but still important groups. Build understanding of their interests, concerns, and change readiness.

- **Create a road map:** Chart the phases, identify performance objectives and measures of success, and focus on priorities and the roll-out process. (Ostroff 2006, pp. 142–143)

What Do the Trends Mean for HR Transformation?

The Transformation in Action example "The U.S. Navy Transformation Initiative" provides the imperative for a global human resource strategy to support corporate global strategy. Human resource professionals must also become "global citizens" and view the global talent pool as the raw material for developing human assets and the global marketplace and technological landscape as their region. This requires a broadening and widening, and sometimes even a dramatic shift in the way we think.

The most successful transformations are those that truly take an enterprise view of the challenge, first looking at the changing environment, the vision, and strategies of the organization to create value in that environment, that is, a holistic view of organizational and people capabilities required for success. All of this must be done with a strong grasp of the implications for cost, timing, and the realities of moving from the current state to the future state.

In more than twenty years of HR experience, the biggest complaint that we hear from businesspeople is that HR does not "get it." Get what?

The U.S. Navy Transformation Initiative
Darrell Ahne, Human Capital Consultant, Hess, Hanna and Associates,
Kevin Odlum, Principal, Clarity Development Group

The authors interviewed two members of the team responsible for the original initiative in the Naval Air Systems Command (NAVAIR), Darrell Ahne, a human capital consultant with Hess, Hanna and Associates, and Kevin Odlum, principal of Clarity Development Group.

The U.S. Navy's Total Force Readiness Transformation Initiative completely reframes how the Navy makes and tracks personnel assignments for everyone in or associated with the Navy. The U.S. Navy operates 276 ships and submarines and more than 4,000 aircraft with a workforce that numbers more than 343,500 active duty personnel, over 100,000 government service civilians, and thousands of contractors providing support services (www.navy.mil).

NAVAIR, headquartered at Patuxent River, Maryland, employs over 30,000 active duty, government-service civilian, and contractor personnel. It provides research, engineering, development, testing and evaluation, acquisition management, and materiel support to the Navy and Marine Corps for aircraft, airborne weapons systems, avionics, and related support areas (www.navy.mil/navydata/organization/org-shor.asp).

Impetus for Change

The Navy's twenty-first century strategic vision is to be "leaner and more capable," requiring dramatic changes in the level of communication and connectivity among all parts of the fleet; the vision also includes the development and acquisition of three new classes of ships, two new aircraft—the joint strike fighter and the V-22—and unmanned aerial and underwater vehicles (Johnson 1997). This transformation also involves reducing the overall workforce significantly.

As the country faced a global War on Terrorism, the resources required to meet the Navy mission of forward presence and operations at a high operational tempo required Navy leadership to consider every aspect of valued contribution and cost—simply put, input of resources and output of mission performance. Ascertaining costs and understanding the technical and business contributions of the total force were made even more complicated by the involvement of active duty military, government-service civilians, and a myriad of large and small defense contractors engaged in each program. The Navy also faced the impending loss of significant numbers of civilian retirees over the next decade. The retirements, combined with the significant workforce reduction, presented a tremendous opportunity to reshape the workforce of the future.

As a result, NAVAIR started asking the following questions:

- How should we think about what people do and how that work is done?

- What do we really need people to do?

- What skills and capabilities will we need twenty to twenty-five years from now?

- How do we build the workforce of the future starting today?

NAVAIR undertook a systematic process at the command level using the following five-step approach:

1. Identify the mission.

NAVAIR reconfirmed the enduring mission of the command to provide aircraft ready for tasking through the acquisition and sustainment of cost-wise current readiness and technically superior future capability to make a great Navy and Marine Corps team better. The clarity of mission and output provided the basis for the application of Continuous Process Improvement tools and methodologies to improve cycle time and output of integrated processes in order to free resources to apply to the most critical skills areas.

2. Baseline the current state.

NAVAIR initiated a baseline analysis that identified how the output of each person in its total workforce of 30,000 (military, civilians, and contractors) connected to an end product (an F-18 aircraft), an intermediate product (a turbine engine), and the associated funding source to track the money flow across programs and functions. Using the task data from an activity-based cost analysis, the project team surveyed each employee to collect input on time spent on each task for each product and funding source. The connections made across the entire workforce were initially analyzed and presented to leadership to engender understanding and begin gap analysis.

3. Categorize skills into competencies.

The next phase was to identify the aggregate skill levels required to complete the work/tasks that contribute to the intermediate and end products. NAVAIR is a competency-aligned organization that assigns the workforce to multidisciplinary integrated product teams in support of naval aviation programs. Technical authority—accountability for the technical integrity and functional career development of the workforce, processes, tools, and outputs—is the role and responsibility of the competency-aligned organization. Competency organizations are composites of major disciplines such as engineering, test and evaluation, logistics, program management, contracts, legal, comptroller, human resources, and command staff administration. With the competency-aligned organization, there is synergy with the needed proficiency and competency of the workforce. An example of a proficiency/competency hierarchy is engineering, structural engineering, advanced materials composite engineering. This ongoing process is leading NAVAIR to a higher level of fidelity surrounding the relationships among skills, competencies, programs, people, and products.

4. Model future competencies and identify and plan to address gaps.

NAVAIR then characterized the subcompetencies that will be needed in the future by modeling skills required by future platforms. For example, F-14s were being phased out of the fleet, and unarmed aerial vehicles (UAVs) were emerging. To continue our example of structural engineering, how can we take what we know about the application of structural engineering subcompetencies on an F-14 and extrapolate that to anticipate what will be needed in the future for a UAV? What gaps and requirements will this cause for jobs and skills in the workplace? What people do we have today who can be prepared to do this work in the future? How do we help people to train for this work and help them take responsibility for their own careers? What new talent will we recruit and for which entities?

5. Determine where the work is best accomplished.

Determine criteria for assignment of work and assess where the work is best accomplished based on criteria of mission risk, cost, and military security. Within the U.S. federal government, some work is deemed as essential military, and other work as inherently civilian governmental. It is necessary to understand and determine the required knowledge, skills, and experience to accomplish the work and then seek the best source for the work within the organization with full consideration of strengths, agility, capability, and ability to assimilate new skills and information. This also caused a shift in thinking about what is required to fill a billet (position). For example, is it right to fill a recruiting billet with a pilot or a nuclear engineer? By better matching the most crucial, constrained, and expensive personnel with work that truly requires those proficiencies/competencies, NAVAIR makes more efficient use of its personnel and maximizes the return on talent development. Today, NAVAIR fills its billets by choosing from the combined proficiencies/competencies for civilians, active duty and reserve military, and contractors.

To institutionalize this effort, Chief of Naval Operations Clark (currently retired) leveraged the Total Force work into his Human Capital Strategy in order to migrate it across the Navy. The objective was to optimize existing resources and manage all cost elements through replicable processes, governance, and communication to maximize the cost effectiveness and quality of service in the way talent is matched to tasks and to use personnel support systems and data management.

HR does not "get" how the business operates and how to develop talent and leadership to help the business grow and prosper. Leaders who were responsible for undertaking the initial pilot programs restructuring the human capital planning succinctly summed up (in an interview with one of the authors) the steps to do this:

First of all, know something about your operations. HR practitioners should at least know what products are produced by their organization and what talent it takes to produce them. Spend some time understanding the value stream of your organization. Create a business decision template that outlines the things that are important for your organization's leaders. Use this template for discussing the implications for all decisions. Act like a consultant. Otherwise, your leaders will bring in the consultants to do the strategic work and you will be reduced to transactions. Soon, more efficient outsourcers with improved system capability will eliminate the need for you to do transactions.

In conclusion, Table 3-2 provides a practical guide to enhancing consulting skills as a human resource leader.

TABLE 3-2

Practical Guide to Being a Human Resource Consultant

1. Learn about your organization:
   - Read the Web page, annual report, press releases, and analyst reports.
   - Study the strategic, marketing, operational, and financial plans.
   - Spend time with customers and in operations.
2. Create and then focus on a vision and the business impact and output of actions.
3. Create a strategic road map or value stream that HR input identifies for human resources.
4. Focus decision making on how what you are proposing adds value to the customer, mission, or company.
5. Create and use good consulting skills:
   - Apply questioning and discovery methodology.
   - Learn facilitation techniques.
   - Create decision templates.
   - Leverage written follow-up and reports to advantage.

4

Future Trends in the General Workforce

To explore coming changes in the workforce and how they relate to, and influence, HR transformation, this chapter identifies two key future workforce trends and asks the following key questions about each:

- What themes underlie the trend?
- What are the likely impacts of the trend?
- How should the impacts of the trend be managed?
- What does the trend mean for HR transformation?

What Are the Key Future Workforce Trends?

Just as product development and marketing strive to exploit emerging desires created by changing customer preferences, human resources should analyze the characteristics, size, and experience of large cohorts in the population to understand the impacts on workforce management. Dramatic shifts in the demographics impact almost everything and underscore the importance of the changing face of the talent pool and the inevitable change in competitive and organizational dynamics. In this chapter, we examine two of most important workforce trends:

- Generational demographics and the resulting impacts on organizational dynamics
- Global shifts in employment and the increasingly global talent pool

We will examine some of the organizational challenges and opportunities presented by these trends.

Generational Demographics

What Themes Underlie the Trend?

For the first time in history, four distinct generations are working together in the United States and Western Europe. Although the definitions of these terms vary depending on the source, they are generally known as the following:

- **Traditionalists, World War II cohort, postwar cohort, Veterans, Silent Generation (those born before 1946):** Key characteristics of the Traditionalists include conformity, traditional values, patriotism, and adversity to risk.

- **Baby boomers (those born between 1946 and 1963):** Key characteristics include individualism, cause orientation, and desire to make a difference. This generation has experienced considerable political and social change, including desegregation and the changing role of women in the workforce and society. The sheer size of this group has had enormous societal and workplace impact for decades and will continue to do so for decades to come.

- **Generation Xers and baby busters (those born between 1964 and 1980):** Key characteristics include self-reliance, independence, informality, and an entrepreneurial nature. This generation has been influenced by dramatic shifts in society, such as two-income households, the prevalence of divorce, and the acceptance of diversity of gender, race, and ethnicity.

- **Millennials, Generation Yers, Digital Natives (those born between 1981 and 2007):** Key characteristics include collaborative team players, respectful of authority, patriotic, and desire physical security. A larger demographic than baby boomers, this group is now entering the workforce in significant numbers. More diverse, globally oriented, and technically savvy than previous generations, this generation will have dramatic impacts on markets, education, and the workplace. (Wikipedia.com, s.v. "Demographics.")

Table 4-1 shows the current makeup of the U.S. workforce. The United States Bureau of Labor Statistics predicts that 25 million people will leave the labor force in the decade 1998–2008. Of this group, 22 million will be forty-five years old or older. In contrast, only 19 million left the labor force during the previous decade. After 2008, as more and more baby boomers reach retirement age, the impact of their retirements will continue to grow. By 2018 all but the youngest baby boomers will be of retirement age. Aggravating the situation is a much smaller pool of workers immediately following the baby boomers. The impact will be somewhat mitigated by many boomers being motivated to stay in the workforce longer by good health as well as by changes in Social Security and increased use of defined contribution pension plans such as 401(k)s, which do not have an age or length-of-service component (Dohm 2000). Nonetheless, human resource professionals must be

TABLE 4-1		
Composition of the U.S. Workforce		
Demographic Cohort	Age Range	Percent of U.S. Workforce
Traditionalist	60–78	10%
Baby Boomer	41–59	46%
Generation X	28–40	29%
Generation Y	Younger than 28	15%

Source: Adapted from K. Columbia, "Addressing Generational Diversity," *Newspapers & Technology,* October 2005.

aware of the potential impact of the loss of sheer numbers, intellectual capital, and the tacit knowledge of the most experienced workers from their workforce. This loss will fuel a global war for talent, especially in the ranks of management and knowledge workers.

When combined with the impact of the leaps of growth in technology, globalization, and increasingly volatile markets, the generational forces contribute to important organizational dynamics. Some people portray the multigenerational workforce as rife with dramatic conflict. However, the title of research compiled in 2006 and published by the Human Resource Planning Society says it all: "The Generation Gap: More Myth than Reality." In fact, all generations highly value the same three employment motivators:

- The success and reputation of their employers

- Engagement of senior management

- The ability to advance their skills and careers (Giancola 2006)

Another similarity across all generations is the desire to work fewer hours, as well as some reluctance to accept promotions that result in greater responsibility. The 2004 Generation and Gender in the Workplace Study conducted by the Families and Work Institute found a dramatic drop between 1992 and 2002 in the desire to accept promotions that would increase levels of responsibility. The decline was greatest among college-educated women of all ages and younger workers of both genders who were looking for better balance of work and family. In 2002, 80 percent of college-educated workers of all ages wanted to work fewer hours than they currently worked (Columbia 2005). In an era when productivity and cost competitiveness are so critical, highly educated workers in many organizations experience a direct conflict between the desire for more flexibility and work–life balance and the need to demonstrate value and improve productivity.

As human resource departments build talent management systems, keeping these motivators and concerns in mind can provide important guidelines for building practices that attract and retain the most desirable employees.

Perhaps the greatest generational impact to organizational dynamics will be in the revolutionary ways in which Digital Natives—people born after 1980 and making up about half of the world's population—

acquire and process information and communicate. The generation that grew up with information technology and connectivity thinks, communicates, and behaves differently than previous generations. Digital Natives are used to multitasking; being connected with one another through instant messaging, cell phones, text messaging, and the Internet; using (and having created) blogging, MySpace, and YouTube to express themselves and share information; and engaging in global virtual collaboration. Digital Natives socialize, play, and interact virtually as naturally as they do face-to-face. They are very comfortable influencing each other, adapting tools, creating networks, and swaying opinions without face-to-face interaction (Prensky 2004). It should be noted that Digital Natives present a global phenomenon, and their characteristics are constant across the globe.

Human resource leaders can take advantage of the comfort with and expectation for virtual connectivity in job, communications, and training design. All leaders should be aware of the viral nature of communications and use them to advantage to accelerate change initiatives. At the same time, this group expects to be involved in decision making and is less influenced by top-down directives. Consider involving Digital Natives on transformation project teams to ensure that plans will address and capture this critical group.

An example of how one organization took advantage of this demographic trend is Capital One, a credit card company that applied the characteristics of Digital Natives and showed what a difference the application of talent can make to a mature industry. Founded in 1995, Capital One is now the fourth-largest credit card provider. Founders Rich Fairbanks and Nigel Morris used statistical data mining to mass-customize credit card offerings ("Everybody's Doing It" 2006). With almost 20,000 employees, Capital One was named to *Fortune*'s "Best Companies to Work For." Capital One uses these same tools to create a positive associate experience in programs such as the following: "Future of Work (FOW) Program that provides flexibility in space, technology and tools for associates to work where and when they need; company-wide support for associates in times of crisis like Hurricanes Katrina and Rita; opportunities to volunteer and give back to the community; and its innovative use of different learning channels for career development like the Audio Learning Program" (Capital One Financial Corporation 2007).

How Should the Impacts of the Trend Be Managed?

Information flows, less hierarchical and more collaborative organizational structures, and the reliance on knowledge sharing have produced a greater need to address the various needs and styles of the generations in talent management and organizational dynamics. Leaders must develop a proactive approach to managing their multigenerational workforce, much the same as they must develop targeted marketing strategies to reach their customer base (VisionPoint n.d.). We suggest doing an audit of the organization, asking such questions as the following:

- What is the generation mix?
- What is the distribution for key functions?
- What risks does this mix present?
- What are the turnover rates, and what can you learn from exit interviews?
- Does the stated culture match the feedback provided by employee surveys and exit interviews?
- Are there pockets of concern or excellence that demonstrate leadership issues or best practices?
- Does the audit reveal alignment or important gaps among cohort groups?
- How well does the workforce match the target customer base?
- What will be the impact of impending retirements on critical knowledge and experience areas?

Consider mapping the workforce by age to determine the generation mix. By asking and analyzing these questions, human resource leaders can identify important gaps and trends in the workforce profile and culture. Any discrepancies should be addressed through changes in policy, communications, training, and recruiting,

Many organizations are pursuing innovative approaches to recruitment. For instance, see the Transformation in Action example "The U.S. Marine Corps Recruiting Command." The United States Marine Corps Recruiting Command (MCRC) provides an exemplar of recruiting, communications, and branding to fulfill changing strategic objectives in the face of major generational demographic changes. Small organizations

The U.S. Marine Corps Recruiting Command
Lieutenant Colonel James Kuhn (Retired)
Advertising and Marketing Branch, U.S. Marine Corps

In 1997, the U.S. Marine Corps published *Warfighting*, which signaled the formal adoption of maneuver warfare as its doctrine. Efforts to operationalize this doctrine serve as a valuable example of a systemwide transformation to adapt to a dynamic environment with new global threats, a changing workforce, and the need to react quickly and decisively to unknown situations. Organizations faced with similar conditions will find it useful to examine and adapt some of the tenets, especially as the transformation relates to talent management and performance development.

The philosophy of Maneuver Warfare is to rapidly and decisively take advantage of emerging situations, using the inherent factors of combat: friction, uncertainty, fluidity, and disorder. In a combat environment, there will be miscommunication, mistakes, and unforeseen events. Success is based on giving the commanders in the field the control to act on emerging events with boldness, surprise, focus, and complementary systems; they also need to be able to target critical vulnerabilities in the opponent. The Marine Corps recognized that mission success would be more likely with swift, decisive action based on actual conditions in the field. The Marine Corps also recognized that such action might be messy but that it would provide more positive results. The Marines recognized that they were not working in a zero-defect environment. There would be mistakes, and they needed to encourage risk taking and decisiveness, as well as good decision making.

To be successful, the Marine Corps needed to change its performance management, called Fitness Reports. Historically, the reviews had been inflated, and as a result officers often gamed the system to advance their subordinates, which meant that truthful marks of average performance became career ending. With the advent of Maneuver Warfare, the Marine Corps recognized that officers needed to be encouraged to take risks without the fear of ruining their careers. The new system required that an officer would review the fitness of his officers as usual. However, in order to create context, the officer was forced to rank the subordinate against all people of that rank that he had ever encountered. The Marine Corps created centralized files comparing all of the officers' fitness reviews and all officers at a given rank. Officers' fitness reviews are compiled up the chain of command in a pyramidal manner so that all officers of a given rank are compared against one another. Each superior officer's reviews are evaluated to minimize a tendency for bias.

Also critical to the success of the Maneuver Warfare doctrine was recruiting individuals with the right perspectives and characteristics. As the Millennials began to come of age and become the target segment, the Marine Corps Recruiting Command (MCRC) recognized that it needed a new recruiting strategy for that generation.

According to Lieutenant Colonel James Kuhn (retired), who headed the advertising and marketing branch for the Marine Corps, the requirements of the Marine Corps drove the development of an integrated marketing and advertising strategy that was designed to attract youth and demonstrate an appreciation for their perspectives and views. Although the fundamental strategy—quality and diversity—for recruiting did not change, the voice of the Marine Corps' advertising did, and everything about the strategy was challenged. The Marine Corps needed young men and women who could meet the challenges of a decentralized operating environment and make decisions that could instantaneously be scrutinized by CNN. That kind of individual has options, and the Marine Corps gladly competed for them with an informed, highly targeted marketing effort that was as sophisticated as that of any brand in the country. The risk of failure was too great; the readiness of the operating forces was dependent on recruiting success, which was a goal of about 38,000 individuals a year. The Marine Corps made recruiting a top priority for resources and assigned only the very best people as recruiters. It was a significant investment that paid off when competition for a shrinking number of interested prospects resulted in the Marine Corps being the only service to consistently meet its recruiting goals. As a footnote, the Marine Corps chose to evaluate and change the strategy while it was enjoying one of its most successful periods of recruiting.

Steps in the Process

1. Assess the environment—risks and opportunities presented by changing conditions
2. Create the vision, mission, and objectives—the Keystone Conference
3. Create and implement the plan—the Recruiting Campaign Plan

MCRC assembled critical stakeholders from all levels, as well as partners in recruiters' sales training and the long-standing advertising partner J. Walter Thompson, for a weeklong session. The agenda included a series of facilitated visioning and strategy sessions interspersed with education by leading academics on strategy and total brand integration and new research from leading experts on the new generation. The Keystone Conference was a success because it allowed new perspectives in the dialogue, candid conflict and discussion on the issues, and, most important, validation on what was sacred and what should be adapted for future success.

The outcome was a framework of strategic objectives that allowed forward movement. Important to note is that the MCRC recognized that it was creating a campaign plan that by necessity would need to be flexible to meet emerging circumstances.

The strategic objectives were:

- Put in place accession goals to provide the numbers of men and women who meet the high-quality and character standards to be successful.

- Ensure that the quality and practices of recruiters are consistent with the brand image, and help to differentiate the Marine Corps from other services—leveraging the Marine Corps' core value and uniqueness—while recognizing that the recruiter is the representative to the community and one of the primary reasons an individual enlists. Evaluate and validate recruiting processes, functions, and recruiting staffing plans. Aggressively pursue policy and process innovations in staffing assignment and logistics as well as recruiting policy. Modernize sales training processes for recruiters.

- Create a cohesive media and communications plan to communicate the brand image and to make all related communications

> consistent with the long-established image of "Smart, Elite Warrior" while still being meaningful to the Millennial generation. Another result of the Keystone Conference was to recognize the increasingly prominent role of influencers—parents, teachers, coaches, and group leaders. The Marine Corps revised its process and materials to appeal to key influencers.
>
> HR leaders can use the steps that the Marine Corps Recruiting Command took to deal with change in their strategy and the simultaneous need to appeal to a new and different generation, the Millennials. Another important lesson from this example is the interrelationship of branding, recruiting, and communications, working together to create an employment and leadership brand. The Marine Corps is an exemplar of an elite leadership brand through the linkage of strategy and mission, relentless consistency in identity, and coordinated communications.

also face special challenges in transforming HR, as illustrated in the Transformation in Action example "The Dynamics of Transforming the HR Function in a Small Organization" on pages 79–82.

One of the most important actions that human resource leaders can take is to ensure that knowledge is captured from the impending upswing of boomer retirees. Perhaps the most important way to manage the trend is to find culturally appropriate and operationally effective ways to capture knowledge from this group. Some potential ideas include sponsoring a "call for papers" on areas of critical expertise; asking experts to deliver brown-bag-lunch-and-learn sessions; creating a mentoring program matching potential retirees with newer employees; capturing presentations, white papers, and reports in a company-wide database; and creating knowledge banks of expertise and competencies.

Another critical step will be to encourage older workers to remain in the workforce or to return to the workforce. To do that, human resource professionals will need to appeal to workers to stay. In 2006 the Human Resource Planning Society published a survey of 1,500 people over age fifty, who were randomly selected from the membership list of CARP (Canada's Association for the 50 Plus). More than 45 percent responded, 327 of whom were retired and 291 of whom were not. Despite differences in retiree status and gender, respondents overwhelmingly (from

57 percent to 92 percent) agreed on the HR practices likely to give them incentive to remain in the workforce or to return to the workforce after retiring. See Table 4-2 for results of the survey.

Although there are significant differences in the responses between groups, the results indicate that mature workers are especially attracted to a culture that values their experience and capabilities. Employers need to demonstrate that they value the experience, knowledge, and skills of older workers. The availability of flexible working options, training and development, job design, performance evaluation practices, and compensation practices is also very important. Human resource professionals need to develop a comprehensive approach that includes human resource practices from all areas targeted to mature workers (Armstrong-Stassen 2006, pp. 42–43).

What Does the Trend Mean for HR Transformation?

The generational demographics will create an impetus for human resource transformation. Clearly a one-size-fits-all traditional approach to compensation, talent and leadership development, and job design and career advancement will not be adequate to address differences in the expectations of emerging generations. Baby boomers have historically been good team players, competitive, and focused on their careers. Generation Xers witnessed their parents undergo corporate downsizing and restructuring; they value flexibility and autonomy, and demand greater work/life balance as well as the opportunity to hone skills that will be useful in the future. Generation Yers are technically sophisticated, excellent team players, and respectful of authority. More than stereotypes, the differences in generations may play out in subtleties of communication and expectations.

The case study "Connecting Across Generations" (pp. 83–85) is a fictionalized example based on actual events. As you read this case study, assume that the HR systems are well designed, strategically aligned, and executed as planned. Consider the following questions: What are the potential generational issues? What are the issues of virtual connectivity? What are the differences in expectations and communication among the various groups? What are the leadership issues? What should the president have done? What would you do as a human resource leader?

TABLE 4-2

HR Practices Providing Most Incentive for Staying in or Returning to the Workforce

	Retired Women (%)	Retired Men (%)	Working Women (%)	Working Men (%)
Recognizing the experience, knowledge, skill, and expertise of mature employees	92	73	74	64
Showing appreciation for a job well done	90	73	71	63
Ensuring that mature employees are treated with respect by others in the organization	89	72	70	61
Conducting performance appraisals so that they fairly and accurately reflect performance and are free from age bias	89	72	67	59
Providing challenging and meaningful tasks or assignments to mature employees	89	71	67	57

Source: Adapted from M. Armstrong-Stassen, "Encouraging Retirees to Return to the Workforce," *Human Resource Planning* 29, no. 4 (2006): 42–43.

The Dynamics of Transforming the HR Function in a Small Organization

Amy Cutter Mulford, Vice President/Chief Financial Officer,
Metro Orlando Economic Development Commission

The Metro Orlando Economic Development Commission (EDC) markets metro Orlando as a location for business expansion and investment. This private, not-for-profit corporation, located in Orlando, Florida, provides a variety of services, which range from site selection and market intelligence to film production permitting and export counseling. Funding comes from private sector members and five local government partners. The annual budget is about $6.5 million, and the EDC has thirty-nine professional employees.

HR Transformation Needed

In 1999 EDC leaders recognized that if the EDC was to remain globally competitive in attracting high-wage, high-value jobs to the region, an organizational transformation was imperative. Having weathered an extensive government audit and the resulting media coverage, they were concerned with improving the company's image in the community and increasing funding, as well as with enhancing the community's reputation as a thriving business location.

Personnel and human resource changes were never a part of the original transformation planning process. In 1999 the EDC had an annual turnover rate of 30 percent and no defined people strategy. Like many small organizations, it had no HR manager or HR department. That responsibility fell under the organization's chief financial officer (CFO), though many of the traditional HR functions were decentralized.

Through the evaluation process, the EDC's leaders quickly realized that the lack of a people strategy was a critical concern and that hiring and keeping the right people would be the difference between being good and becoming world-class. Economic development is, above all, a "relationship industry"; the people who work on the EDC's behalf to effectively market the community are irreplaceable keys to success.

The First Steps in This Process

The first step was to better understand why people at all levels of the organization were leaving. The EDC was generally losing people to for-profit companies. Although they indicated commitment to the work of the EDC, workers cited two reasons for departure in exit interviews: low salaries and poor benefits. At that time, like companies nationwide, the EDC was facing skyrocketing health insurance premiums, and that burden was shared with employees. Not only was it difficult to keep employees, the organization was virtually unable to attract a candidate who was the sole supporter of a family because the premiums were so high.

In 2000, the EDC hired two consultants to help address and improve turnover: a compensation consultant and an HR consultant. The compensation consultant provided competitive data on appropriate salaries for the industry, as well as grade and salary range structures for all positions. This led to the development of a two-year strategy to bring underpaid employees up to their market rate, a strategy that was quickly and fully communicated to the staff.

The HR consultant conducted a confidential written employee satisfaction survey of all employees; then the consultant met individually with each employee to collect direct feedback. The results of that survey were surprising. Although salaries made the top three on the list, benefits were of greater concern than pay. Most surprising was the top item on the list, which was unrelated to compensation. The staff felt that they were working in "silos," with ten managers running ten separate and often competing divisions. They felt that this created unnecessary inconsistency and expressed interest in being part of a united organization where everyone worked together to meet shared goals.

What Worked and What Didn't Work

The next two years were spent researching solutions to these issues, as well as working to increase the organization's overall funding. EDC engaged an MBA consulting team from Orlando-based Rollins College, which provided its services at no cost. Together EDC and the team researched alternatives and determined that outsourcing was the best alternative to improving benefits while controlling associated costs.

In 2002 financial constraints led to a restructuring that eliminated six staff positions. Though restructuring is always a difficult time for an organization, especially one so small, EDC was able to turn the restructuring into an opportunity to transform the organization. Today that transitional period is viewed as a turning point with long-term positive impacts for the EDC.

Concurrent with the restructuring decision, management obtained board approval to partner with a professional employer organization (PEO) that would provide the underlying HR services. While maintaining control over people strategy, EDC utilized the expertise of the PEO's HR specialist to improve its human resource processes. Over the course of two years, while retraining management and staff each step of the way, the organization reinvented each component of its HR function:

- Compensation and incentive plan
- Benefits
- Corporate vision/culture
- Recruitment strategy
- Retention strategy
- Performance management system
- Training and professional development
- Payroll processing
- Policies, procedures, documentation, and metrics

In addressing benefits, the PEO partnership provided employees with a stable and affordable Fortune 500–quality benefits package. These HR improvements created consistency across all EDC departments, brought financial relief to some, and provided a boost in morale to all.

In a move to create a more-unified organization, the basis of the EDC's small annual incentive plan was changed from focusing on individual departmental goals to achievement of company-wide goals. While EDC, as a not-for-profit, is limited in its ability to compete with for-profit companies on salary, it could now effectively compete on benefits and the other components of a solid HR function.

There is also a "psychological paycheck" associated with work in the nonprofit, community-building realm. Another important step was to clarify and rally around a shared vision. To do that the whole organization participated in a study of Jim Collins' Good to Great theory. The organization then went through a process, first with the management team and later with the entire staff, to clearly define its raison d'être: growth in high-wage, high-value jobs, and capital investment—with the end result being increased opportunity and prosperity for the community's children and grandchildren. This passion or "righteous mission" has since become a filter in EDC's hiring and evaluation processes.

Where the Organization Stands Now

Board members and clients often ask how EDC is able to attract such a dedicated, dynamic, and diverse group of bright and committed people. The Metro Orlando EDC is now recognized in the community as a great place to work.

Since 2002 turnover has dropped dramatically and is now hovering between 5 and 8 percent annually. Today most of the turnover is either related to lack of opportunity for advancement or a hiring mistake. In a small organization, opportunities for advancement within the organization are often limited. The leaders know that, and they plan for it. They strive for continuous improvement in the hiring process to limit hiring mistakes.

EDC continues to measure employee satisfaction every other year. It also reviews and updates both its policies and its salary structure every two to three years.

How the Transformation Helped the Organization Fulfill Its Goals

The ability to recruit and retain effective staff at all levels of the organization has affected every standard by which EDC measures effectiveness. Between 1999 and 2006, EDC revenues grew by 69 percent. Metro Orlando has received numerous accolades from business publications that have touted the community as a hub for modeling simulation and training, digital media and entertainment technologies, and biotech. Most important, EDC has been instrumental in bringing new companies into the community and in helping local companies grow. These companies create the jobs necessary to improve the regional economy.

Case Study
Connecting Across Generations

As president of the technical consulting division of a large company, John, age fifty, had the challenge of generating profitable double-digit growth and expanding into new target market industries. John was proud of his division's financial and operational performance. However, he knew that he needed to enhance the firm's client focus and creativity in proposing client solutions, especially in the use of technology and mixed media. The division was an amalgamation of legacy organizations with a large number of long-term employees, many whom had worked together for decades.

John recruited Will (age forty-five) as the new leader of Client Solutions and several new key leads (all age forty and under) for client development, relationship management, and solutions development roles. At the same time, he reorganized and promoted Clay (age fifty-five) to a senior role as Operations manager with control over schedule, budget, and assignment of people resources. John talked a lot about fostering a creative culture. He gave Will explicit directions to bring the "voice of the customer" into the organization and to "shake it up," and he said that he did not mind conflict in his organization. At the same time, John asked Clay to improve the predictability and program management oversight of all projects. Clay increased his staff (primarily with long-time employees) and imposed more stringent reporting requirements for all projects. Under the new structure, the Solution lead and the Operations lead would colead projects with joint responsibility for deliverables, budget, and schedule. Key resources in technology, media, and development reported directly to a functional leader assigned in a matrix to the project teams, which were made up of a mix of full-time employees and freelance contractors.

Will was an entrepreneur with a background in advertising and marketing, and was full of great new ideas and solutions. With a gregarious personality, Will was described by one of his peers as a "boomer who looks like a Gen Xer and thinks like a Millennial." Will brought an unprecedented level of creativity to the Solution space. He also pushed his team to increase their creativity and strategic approach with their clients. He was vocal about his team members' developmental needs. He instituted a client strategic planning process, increased revenue goals for all of his direct reports, and gave pointed feedback to his staff. Will focused his time on client interface, relied heavily on virtual communication with his team, permitted flexible working arrangements, and at the same time expected his team to be collaborative and connected in sharing ideas to generate creative solutions for the clients.

Clay ran his team with stringent rules and relied heavily on face-to-face staff meetings and project reviews for coordination. He required formal plans and frequent project updates. Clay frequently stated that the only way for a team to be integrated was to meet each morning and plan the day's events.

Conflict between the two leaders and their teams was evident from the beginning. In the project teams, both the Solution lead and the Operations lead were vying for control and decision-making authority. Will complained that the Project leads were too process oriented and rigid. Will and his team grew frustrated when new ideas, tools, and solutions were "slowed by process requirements." Clay complained that the Solution leads were too client-focused, did not attend meetings, and lacked process discipline. Team members on both sides grew frustrated. At times, client requirements were not met because of the differences on how to proceed among the project teams. On more than one occasion, Will and Clay erupted in loud vehement arguments that were heard throughout the office. John responded by saying that he deliberately created the conflict in the system and needed both of the leaders to play the role they were playing. He asked them to try to get along a little better.

The performance management system was well designed and robust. Goals were aligned with a flow-down of growth, financial, customer, people, and productivity goals from the CEO through the division head to leaders to individual contributors. Salary, bonus, and stock grants were based on a combination of corporate, division, team, and individual performance. At review time, both leaders received an "exceeds expectations" performance rating and sizable bonuses and grants. Leaders were expected to do an annual 360-feedback process that included leaders, peers, direct reports, and clients.

After reviewing Will's feedback with him in a coaching session, Will's coach commented that it was the most interesting feedback he had ever seen and that he did not know how to advise him on it. Client feedback demonstrated that they appreciated the creativity and innovation but that sometimes the project teams did not execute on commitments. Peers either lauded Will's energy and ideas or complained that he was a "loose cannon." Feedback from Will's team was also split between those who loved his style and creativity and those who wanted more structure and felt he pushed them too hard. A couple of comments alleged that there were favorites on the team. Other comments described the conflict between the two leaders and the resulting project team conflict. One comment described the working environment as the most toxic the employee had ever experienced. John's comments included a statement that he was aware that there was controversy but felt that Will knew who the players were.

Over the next few months, Will and many of the new Solution leads left the organization. John reorganized and put Clay's group clearly in charge of projects. Client feedback has been mixed, and the loss of capability is evident.

Might this situation occur in your organization? What are some of the dynamics in expectations for leadership, communication, and work styles that are occurring in your environment? Consider using this case to draw out insights from various groups in your workplace.

Lori Bradley, a leader of talent management and organization development for a business employing 13,000 people in the aerospace industry, underscores the urgency of human resource transformation in the face of generational demographics: "Talent management is a big area of emphasis for us right now. With the aging workforce and the fiercely competitive labor market in our industry, it is critical that we take proactive steps to ensure we have the right talent in the right roles at the right time." In an interview, Bradley elaborated:

We now have four generations in the workforce simultaneously. This presents some unique challenges in how we approach training, reward systems, work-life balance, change management, technology adoption, and so forth. The aging of the baby boomer generation also creates a need to carefully manage and mitigate retirement risk through effective succession planning and systems of knowledge transfer. Acceleration pools are becoming a popular tool to address the need to bring people along quickly and prepare them to assume leadership roles quicker and earlier than we might have been comfortable with in the past. Strategic Talent Management cuts across areas to integrate HR systems and management, learning and development, organization development, organizational effectiveness, succession planning, talent acquisition, and workforce shaping, . . . all driven by business strategic drivers. A talent manager's job today is to translate strategic needs into leadership and key talent capabilities, and to ensure the appropriate systems are in place to develop and retain that key talent.

Working as a strategic business partner to set organizational strategy and direction, Bradley emphasizes to executive leadership, "We must find ways to accelerate the development of our people. We must get them ready for more responsibility—faster. We simply do not have the luxury of having the next generation of technical people and leaders go through the same experiences, job rotations, and 'pay their dues' the same way that you did." Bradley adds that this is a great time for human resource people to shine. "Human resources is easy to ignore when there are plenty of resources. The current environment demands that human resource leaders demonstrate value through organization design, talent development, and organization effectiveness."

Human resource leaders in the multigenerational and virtually connected workforce must focus on leading change and creating organizational processes that allow each individual to contribute to overall performance. Creating opportunities for collaboration and a clear contribution to the overall good is important. As always, setting tangible, actionable goals will be paramount. Additionally, human resource leaders will need to be sure that expectations of office workers and virtual workers are clear and reflect the needs of the business and not necessarily the preferences of individual managers. Top-down, hierarchical structures and requirements for in-person communications will be increasingly less successful.

Global Talent

Next we will examine the global war on talent and the internationalization of talent markets. As markets and companies become increasingly international, so does the talent pool. In this section, we examine some of the forces behind this trend, attempt to separate the reality from the myth, and provide suggestions on how to deal with the trends.

What Themes Underlie the Trend?

Companies have become much bigger and more global. The magnitude of the trend and the need for talent is exemplified by the following examples: "Global spending on IT outsourcing is estimated to increase from $193 billion in 2004 to $260 billion in 2009" ("The World Is Our Oyster" 2006, p. 2). Global revenue earned by professional services firms grew from $390 billion in 1990 to $911 billion in 2000 ("Everybody's Doing It" 2006, p. 1). Today, McKinsey boasts eighty-six locations in forty-six countries (www.mckinsey.com/aboutus/locations).

Astute companies are taking advantage of local knowledge to best develop and market products to local markets. Local employees are better able to understand the demands and constraints of the local economy, such as real wages, home size, availability of electricity, and storage space. Multinational firms are also forming global R&D teams to take advantage of around-the-clock availability, leverage national clusters of excellence, deal with differences in regulations, and give access to research laboratories in universities ("The World Is Our Oyster" 2006, p. 3).

For example, General Electric Company (GE) predicts that approximately 60 percent of its revenues will come from international markets by 2010. GE's fastest growing markets are China, India, the Middle East, and Eastern Europe, with growth rates in these areas approaching 20 percent a year. With half of its 320,000 employees already outside of the United States, GE will continue to shift production to take advantage of lower cost operations, to align revenue production with cost incurrence, and to mitigate the risk of unfavorable economic conditions in a particular country (Christoffersen 2007). Currently, GE boasts 2,500 researchers at four multidisciplinary facilities around the world in Niskayuna, New York; Bangalore, India; Shanghai, China; and Munich, Germany. GE

Global Research is made up of ten global laboratories organized by scientific disciplines, all focused on leveraging technology breakthroughs across multiple GE businesses. Each lab is cosmopolitan, with people from the United States, Europe, China, and India collaborating and building on one another's successes (www.ge.com/research).

The human resource implications include the need to develop globally and train people on the use of virtual collaboration tools, project management skills, and the need to understand and adapt to local differences.

The cost pressures of the changing demographics and demands of the labor force for labor savings as well the opening of markets and the movement toward more nontraditional roles, contingent workforces, and outsourcing are some of the factors behind the global war for talent. Consider the difference in the average hours worked by workers from different countries. As illustrated by Table 4-3, American workers put in on average almost 20 percent fewer hours than their Indian counterparts, while German workers averages 27 percent fewer hours. When combined with higher wages and benefit costs, the difference is dramatic.

Global outsourcing is creating a boom in India and China, and there is fear in the United States and Europe that all the best-paying jobs in both services and manufacturing will migrate to the developing world. There is also a fear that America and Europe will not be able to retain talent. In a large-scale global study, the McKinsey Global Institute determined that constraints of weak infrastructure, inaccessibility to employment centers and transportation, and uneven educational systems will limit the number of service jobs moving offshore to levels far lower than have been feared. Only 13 percent of the talent in the developing world have the education, culture, and language skills needed to work for a Western multinational. To put the job shift into perspective, the number of service jobs moving offshore is projected to rise from 1.5 million in 2003 to 4.1 million in 2008. The estimate of 4.1 million constitutes 1.2 percent of the labor force in the developed world. We can compare this number with the magnitude of job change in the United States, where 4.6 million American workers start with a new employer every month ("Nightmare Scenarios" 2006).

The rapid growth in China and India has resulted in talent shortages, especially in a lack of senior and middle managers. In China, two out of three companies report difficulties in hiring senior management.

TABLE 4-3	
Work Hours in the United States and Other Countries	
Country	Average Hours Worked per Year
India	2,350
United States	1,900
Germany	1,700

Source: Adapted from "The World Is Our Oyster: The Talent War Has Gone Global and So Have Talent Shortages," *Economist,* October 5, 2006.

In both India and China, the demographic group that would typically assume such roles grew up in the old state-dominated systems. Both Indian and Chinese companies continue to recruit Western managers and pay heavily for strong management skills. The average pay increase for IT project managers in India has been 23 percent a year over the past four years ("The World Is Our Oyster" 2006).

America still has overwhelming advantages in the global war for talent: the quality of its universities, the business environment, management talent, and willingness to pay for quality people. Additionally, the capital markets' access to venture capital will continue to propel a positive employment environment. Although the European Union is more burdened by regulations and invests 30 percent less in research and development than is the case in the United States, it is attempting to reform immigration laws to attract more talent. Europe also has tacit expertise, such as German engineering, Italian design, and Finnish wireless technology, that is highly valued in the knowledge economy ("Nightmare Scenarios" 2006).

What Are the Likely Impacts of the Trend?

Germany, France, Ireland, Britain, and many other governments are easing restrictions on visas to attract skilled workers. Canada and Australia are offering incentives. Singapore may have the most ambitious program, one in which only 3 percent of companies report difficulties with immigration issues as opposed to rates of 24 percent in China and 46 percent in the United States ("Opening the Doors" 2006).

Companies facing competitive global markets are determined to keep their wage costs down. At the same time, these same companies are determined to keep their best talent. As a result, the companies are willing to take special measures to keep top talent and are increasingly willing to pay compensation differentials. According to a Society for Human Resource Management Survey, the percentage of companies willing to take special measures to retain their top talent rose from 35 percent in 2004 to 49 percent in 2005. A similar survey by the Corporate Executive Board found that 88 percent of organizations wanted to increase pay differentials. The survey found that variance in performance increases with job complexity. For example, the best computer programmers are at least twelve times more productive than those with average skills ("The Revenge of the Bell Curve" 2006).

How Should the Impacts of the Trend Be Managed?

First and foremost, human resource leaders need to understand their organization's global strategy and operational footprint. Then they must match this strategy with a global staffing strategy. Human resource professionals and other leaders would do well to adapt some of the following measures to enhance their talent management ("Everybody's Doing It" 2006):

Identify the critical talent

- What are the most important jobs?
- Where are these jobs located?
- What capabilities, skills, knowledge, and attitudes do we need to do them?
- What are the biggest problems with the positions: turnover, lack of skilled candidates, cost?
- What components of the job are most unattractive? What could be done in another way?

Plan ahead

- Anticipate upcoming requirements based on future strategy and product/service offerings.
- Anticipate important changes in location.

- Anticipate retirements and potential skills gaps.
- Identify critical skills.
- Inventory and collect key knowledge and skills.
- Involve leaders and key knowledge holders in succession planning.

Identify and attract key talent not in the job market

- Network at industry conferences and professional associations.
- Pay attention to "stars" from competing firms.
- Perform Internet searches for patents, publications, and speaking engagements.
- Create internal talent markets.
- Encourage employees to apply for jobs across the organization.
- Provide visibility and new challenges brought about by high-profile project work.
- Provide mentors and ambassadors to new managers and new recruits.

What Does the Trend Mean for HR Transformation?

The human resource and leadership challenge to compete in the global talent war is to provide world-class leadership by finding, recruiting, and training top talent in the right places; by managing innovation; and by allowing localization while maintaining a strong corporate culture. Human resource leaders are in the unique position to develop, nurture, and communicate what it means to work for a particular organization. Creating what is called the "leadership brand" or the "employment value proposition" is very similar to creating a brand proposition for the company's market and should include defining the following to the employees and target demographics of the talent market:

- Company culture and values and, most important, how it feels day-to-day to work there
- Company growth goals and how employees will benefit from contributing to that growth
- Compensation, health, and retirement benefits

- Opportunities for career growth and skills development
- Opportunities for exciting projects and advancement

And like marketing professionals creating a branding strategy, human resource professionals must communicate their leadership brand internally and externally. They must also be aware of discrepancies, celebrating diversity and winning awards for their programs rather than having women or minorities find the organization culture difficult and leave in droves. Critically important is developing a network of current and former employees to recruit and champion desirable talent. Of course, the closer the company's reality is to its leadership brand or employment value proposition, the more successful it will be. Human resource leaders should be especially cognizant of the power of connecting branding with communications and people development. Every communication is an opportunity to train on the brand proposition, and carefully trained employees reflect the brand in every action.

5

Transforming HR by Focusing on Future Trends

....

This chapter centers on transforming human resources by identifying ten top future HR trends and asking these key questions about each:

- What causes the trend?
- What are the likely impacts of the trend?
- What does the trend mean for HR transformation?

What Are the Key Future Trends?

Examining trends—and especially workforce and HR trends—is a perennially popular activity. After all, the trends that influence HR also dramatically influence organizations. They do not stay the same nationally; nor do they remain exactly the same globally. According to the Society for Human Resource Management's *2006–2007 Workplace Forecast,* the top ten HR trends are:

1. Rising health care costs

2. Increased use of offshoring

3. Threat of increased health care/medical costs on U.S. competitiveness

4. Increased demand for work–life balance

5. Retirement of large numbers of baby boomers

6. New attitudes toward aging and retirement as baby boomers reach retirement age

7. Rise in the number of individuals and families without health insurance

8. Increase in identity theft

9. Work intensification as employers try to increase productivity with fewer employees

10. Vulnerability of technology to attack or disaster

These trends may be properly regarded as macrotrends, meaning that they have an impact on many different organizations and functions across global markets. In HR, microtrends would have an impact on specific HR functional areas and specific organizations, functions, or industries. To discover those microtrends, look at the specific research conducted for HR functions, organizations, industries, or functional areas such as accounting, management information systems, production/operations, or marketing.

The macrotrends do not mean the same thing in all settings. As a matter of fact, the meaning of each trend may vary by nation, industry, organization, or even functional area within an organization. But it is worth describing their general meanings. Trends stem from complex causes, and few, if any, workforce trends have only one root cause. The world is much too complex for that. Indeed, most trends have multiple drivers and many root causes. And, in many cases, the causes of one trend influence—or even cause—others.

Trend #1: Rising Health Care Costs

Aggregate health expenditures in the United States, as a share of U.S. Gross Domestic Product (GDP), have risen from about 5 percent in 1960 to nearly 14 percent in recent years. These expenditures could top 17 percent of GDP by 2011, thus rising to about $9,216 per person per year. This figure would represent a doubling in per capita spending on health care in the United States since 2000 ("Nearly $3 Trillion" 2002). Drug prescriptions are a key driver in health costs, notes Zwiljich (2006).

Causes

There is no single root cause for rising health care costs, but some of the multiple causes include lack of governmental leadership to address the cost of health care, the escalating cost of medical technology, the research and development costs of launching new drugs, and differing global policies and value systems underlying medical care.

Likely Impacts

Rising health care costs are likely to lead to increasing government regulation to require individuals to carry insurance. They are also likely to cause fewer employers to provide health insurance—unless a law is passed to require employers to do so. They are also likely to lead to efforts by individuals to find ways to avoid paying for health insurance. Indeed, some crime may be stimulated by the need to pay for the high cost of medical care, especially when catastrophically expensive procedures are needed.

What the Trend May Mean for HR Transformation

Corporate leaders would like to see HR take a role in the effort to contain health care costs. HR will need to take the lead in finding creative ways to contain health care costs; one of those ways could be to encourage wellness.

Trend #2: Increased Use of Offshoring

U.S. companies were expected to spend approximately $17.6 billion on offshore outsourcing in 2005. That was a jump from $5.5 billion the year before ("Offshore Outsourcing Increasing" 2001). Of course, *outsourcing* means sending work outside a firm; *offshoring* means sending work offshore; and *offshore outsourcing* means sending work outside a firm and offshore from the firm that initiates the work. "Twelve percent of outsourcing spending in 2005 will involve offshore resources, growing to 19 percent in 2009," noted Saugatuck (2005, p. 1). "Less than one-third of companies surveyed agreed that potential backlash against their company's brand is impacting their offshore outsourcing decisions. And less than one-third agreed that consideration of the potential impact on their home country's economy is impacting their offshore outsourcing decision" (Saugatuck 2005, p. 1).

HR functions are particularly prone to outsourcing. Rice (2005, p. 1) cites a study that "estimates that 85 percent of U.S. enterprises will outsource at least one component of their HR functions. The most popular areas for outsourcing are non-core, back-office services such as payroll, benefits, and education and training. The HR business process outsourcing market will grow from $25 billion in 2002 to $38 billion in 2007, an 8.6 percent compound annual growth rate."

Causes

Offshore outsourcing decisions are driven by many considerations. Cost, although the best-known rationale for offshore outsourcing, is not the only reason for it. Other rationales include desires to expand into international markets, expand global expertise, and avoid escalating U.S. benefits costs. Another is the desire to acquire new expertise by tapping talent outside a firm or even outside a given national setting.

The Software Engineering Institute ("Why Do Organizations Outsource" 2006) lists ten reasons that organizations outsource their work:

- Reduce and control operating costs
- Improve company focus
- Gain access to world-class capabilities
- Free internal resources for other purposes
- Gain resources not available internally
- Accelerate reengineering benefits
- Improve function difficult to manage or out of control
- Make capital funds available

- Share risks
- Obtain cash infusion

Likely Impacts

The increased use of offshoring is likely to lead individuals and government bodies to become more aware of which employers are using offshoring. There have been calls to require some employers to sell only American-made products or sell products in America that were made in America. But that is a difficult requirement to police in a global economy in which multinational firms may work across borders with impunity.

What the Trend May Mean for HR Transformation

HR professionals need to find ways to justify their existence. HR must demonstrate excellent and cost-effective service. An effective mix of HR services could mean that some HR services are outsourced and that other than full-time staff get HR work accomplished.

Trend #3: Threat of Increased Health Care/ Medical Costs on U.S. Competitiveness

Rice (2005, p. 1) points out that "since U.S. companies compete with many overseas companies that do not offer employer-sponsored health-care programs," health care and medical costs could have a profoundly negative impact on U.S. global competitiveness. "According to the Department of Labor," notes Rice, "although increases in wages and salaries continued to be moderate, benefit costs continued to rise more rapidly in 2004. Wages and salaries increased by about 2 percent over the last year while benefit costs increased by over 6 percent."

Consider the following facts about health care costs (Adams 2005, p. 1):

- The No. 1 problem facing all U.S. employers today is the skyrocketing cost of health insurance.

- Rated as the No. 1 problem facing all U.S. employers by the Society for Human Resource Management, the cost of health care was recently mentioned in a front-page story about a projected sharp decline in General Motors' expected 2005 profits.

- GM is the largest private provider of health insurance in America; it spent $5.2 billion in 2004 on health insurance for its retirees, employees, and their families.

- While many people may not be directly affected by GM's plight, the effects of the health care insurance crisis are insidious enough to be felt almost everywhere.

- For example, the National Association of Independent Colleges and Universities estimated tuition increases ranged from 5.5 percent to 6 percent in the nation's colleges and universities in 2004.

- Health insurance cost increases for faculty and staff are a major factor in tuition increases each year that far exceed the annual inflation rate.

- Consider also that a major reason for downsizing businesses in the United States and for the wholesale offshoring of American jobs to countries like China and India is not so much lower wages as lower health insurance costs.

- Whereas large private employers are the major providers of health care coverage, small businesses typically do not provide coverage because they cannot afford it.

- In 2002–2003, 36.7 percent of all children in the United States—that amounts to 27 million people younger than 18—lived with families that could not afford health insurance.

- Approximately one in three Americans over age 65—that amounts to about 82 million people—lacked health insurance for all or part of 2002–2003, the most recent year for which statistics are available.

- Government leaders must take the lead, mediate among the parties, and devise workable plans that probably will not satisfy everyone completely.

The escalating cost of health care in the United States has had several results. One is that organizations are passing on an increasing share of health insurance costs to employees, thereby eroding individuals' real earnings. Another is that organizations are passing on increases in health insurance costs to retirees, which may prompt some individuals to delay retirement. A third result is that organizations and individuals are taking wellness and healthy living efforts more seriously than ever before.

Causes

The escalating cost of health care in the United States is one cause for plant shutdowns and the so-called deindustrialization of America. Many firms move offshore to avoid paying benefits costs associated with their workers. This flight of jobs, in turn, threatens U.S. global competitiveness.

Likely Impacts

As the American public becomes more aware of just how much the threat of increased health care and medical costs threatens U.S. competitiveness, demands are likely to increase that governmental efforts and regulations be established to deal with the problem. Some of those efforts may be wise. Others may be ill-advised.

What the Trend May Mean for HR Transformation

National trends cannot be addressed solely by individual employers, but employer trends can be addressed by individual employers. HR practitioners should be asking people in their organizations how the costs of health care can be contained or reduced.

Trend #4: Increased Demand for Work–Life Balance

Individuals are increasingly seeking a balance between their personal and work lives, commonly known as *work–life balance*. A key reason for it is that, in the wake of decades of cost cutting and downsizing, organizations have too few workers chasing too much work.

In the year 2000, the Institute for Employment Research, University of Warwick, and IFF Research in the United Kingdom studied the opinions of 2,500 employers and 7,500 employees. The research concluded that many employees seek work–life balance. About one in nine full-time employees work more than sixty hours a week, and "two-thirds of male employees believe that part-time working would damage their career prospects" ("Work–Life Balance" 2000). Additional findings noted in the study were these:

- 80 percent of workplaces had employees who worked more than their standard hours, with 39 percent doing so without extra pay.

- Just 20 percent of employers were fully aware of increased maternity leave rights, and 24 percent fully aware of new paternal leave rights.

- 25 percent of entitled female employees took less than 18 weeks maternity leave.

- 55 percent of employers consider it acceptable to allow staff to move from full-time to part-time work in some cases.

- 24 percent of employees now work flextime with 12 percent working only during school terms.

- 56 percent of women preferred flexible working—for example, part-time or home-based—after a pregnancy to having a longer maternity leave period.

Leaders of organizations are demanding more from workers in an effort to squeeze greater productivity at reduced cost from smaller groups of employees, a condition leading to so-called *schizophrenic organizations* that say one thing ("employees are our greatest assets") but do conflicting things ("our workers must work harder and longer") (Wentworth 2002). The result is unyielding pressure to put work before family, a condition leading not only to increasing social fragmentation and divorce but also to increasing stress, with results such as drug abuse, alcoholism, and even white-collar crime.

Causes

Employers' desire to save money on wages and benefits leads them to downsize, offshore, and outsource work. The remaining employees are thus pressured even more to perform. One predictable side effect is that workers demand more ability to put their individual and family needs in perspective—that is, in balance—with employer needs.

Likely Impacts

One likely impact of increased demand for work–life balance is to explore more flexible ways to perform work. Much work can be performed virtually, and that ability may lead to increased use of telecommuting and of nontraditional workers to provide work from home or from international settings. That trend, in turn, may help to address the increased demand for work–life balance.

What the Trend May Mean for HR Transformation

HR practitioners should take the lead in building work–life balance programs. Many such programs exist, and best practices have been identified for such programs.

Trend #5: Retirement of Large Numbers of Baby Boomers

Dohm (2000, p. 1) discusses the impact of the aging of the labor force:

> As the age of the U.S. labor force increases, a greater number of people will leave the labor force due to death, disability, or retirement. Of the 25 million people projected by the Bureau of Labor Statistics to leave the labor force between 1998 and 2008, 22 million will be aged 45 years or older, and thus will be leaving mostly to retire. The total number of people who left the labor force the previous decade was 19 million. Over the 1998–2008 period, the oldest baby boomers will be aged 52 to 62. After 2008, as more and more baby boomers reach retirement age, the impact of their retirements will continue to grow.

It is fair to ask *so what?* There are really many answers, but the danger is that there will be too few well-qualified workers to meet the needs of the U.S. economy, thereby driving up wages, hastening the deindustrialization of the United States and the European Union, and making it tougher to retain talented workers. At the same time, economists worry that huge numbers of retirees may strain pension benefits, health care, and other social services (Cauchon and Waggoner 2004).

Cause

The cause of this trend is that large numbers of people—the so-called baby boomers—are reaching traditional retirement age. Many will retire; others will not, and they may reshape the workplace as they work past the traditional retirement age in flexible working arrangements.

Likely Impacts

The retirement of large numbers of baby boomers will be likely to focus attention on talent management efforts designed to attract, retain, and develop qualified talent to meet future organizational needs. It may also lead to creative ways to perform the work and to tap the retiree work-force to achieve work results.

What the Trend May Mean for HR Transformation

HR practitioners should focus attention on preparing their organizations for large-scale retirements. This is particularly true in organizations with long-service employees. HR practitioners should take the lead in establishing and implementing effective succession planning and talent management programs.

Trend #6: New Attitudes Toward Aging and Retirement as Baby Boomers Reach Retirement Age

As baby boomers near traditional retirement age in the United States and in other nations, the sheer size of their generation poses unique challenges for members of the generation, for policy makers, and for employers. Some experts predict labor shortages, changes in immigration policies to attract younger workers, and negative impacts on Social Security and Medicare, private health care insurance, prescription drug reimbursement policy for retirees, and many other issues.

Baby boomers may not be able to retire in as genteel a style as they would like. Instead, many may be forced to work full-time or part-time as a result of inadequate personal financial planning and insufficient funding for promised benefits by governments and by businesses.

The Urban Institute (2006, pp. 1–2) reported the followiing on labor force trends among older Americans:

- The number of adults age 25 to 54, who have traditionally accounted for the bulk of the nation's workforce, will remain virtually unchanged at about 125 million between 2000 and 2020 as the overall adult population grows by about 46 million.

- Older men are less likely to work today than in previous generations, when jobs were more physical, health problems more prevalent, and life expectancy shorter. Only 53 percent of men 62 to 64 were in the labor force in 2005, down from 76 percent in 1963.

- Falling retirement ages and rising life expectancy mean that Americans are now spending more time in retirement than ever before. Between 1950 and 2002, the average age that people started collecting Social Security fell from 68.5 to 63.6 years. As a result, men now average about 17.1 years in retirement, up from 11.7 years in 1950. Women, on average, spend about 21.4 years in retirement, compared with only 13.5 years in 1950.

- The older population provides probably the best source of additional workers to fuel the economy.

- An influx of older people into the workforce would ease the labor shortage created by an aging population. If current rates continue, the number of workers per nonworking adult 65 and older will fall from 4.5 to 3.3 between 2000 and 2020. However, if men 55 and older work at the same rate as they did in 1950, while other men and all women work at their 2000 rates, then the ratio would fall only to 4.1 in 2020.

- Workers who delay retirement earn more money, accumulate additional Social Security, and build more wealth in employer-sponsored pensions. Working longer also extends retirement savings, reducing the years over which Social Security, pensions, and other wealth are spread. Urban Institute simulations show that delaying retirement by five years would enable individuals, on average, to increase annual retirement spending by 56 percent.

- If all workers delayed retirement by five years, the additional Social Security taxes would offset more than half of the Social Security shortfall projected for 2045. The additional government revenue from both income taxes and Social Security payroll taxes would far exceed the size of the Social Security deficit.

- Several recent studies suggest that working longer improves people's physical health and emotional well-being. Ninety-seven percent of employed adults age 70 and older report that they enjoy going to work.

- Reversing a century-long trend, older men are now working more than they did a few years ago. Between 1995 and 2005, the labor force participation rate for men 62 to 64 increased from 45 to 53 percent. Male participation rates decline with age, falling in 2005 from 75 percent at ages 55 to 61, to 53 percent at ages 62 to 64, to 34 percent at ages 65 to 69, and to 14 percent at age 70 and older. About 12.6 million men 55 and older were working in 2005, including 2.9 million age 65 and older.

- Possible explanations for the recent increase in work at older ages include Social Security reforms, changes in employer-sponsored benefits, improvements in health, and declines in physical job demands. Congress raised the eligibility age for full Social Security benefits (from 65 for those born before 1938 to 67 for those born after 1959), increased the rate at which monthly payments rise with delayed benefits, and eliminated the benefit reduction for those working beyond the full retirement age. Also, many employers have replaced traditional pensions with 401(k)–type plans, which (unlike most traditional plans) tend to increase in value when older workers remain on the job. Many employers are also dropping retiree health plans, discouraging retirement before Medicare begins.

- Older workers are most likely to be college educated and in good health. In 2002, 17 percent of adults 70 and older with some college were working, compared with 11 percent of those with a high school diploma and 9 percent of those who did not complete high school. Eighteen percent of adults 70 and older in excellent or very good health were working in 2002, compared with only 6 percent of those in fair or poor health.

- Self-employment increases dramatically with age. About 36 percent of working men 70 and older were self-employed in 2004, compared with 24 percent at age 62 to 64 and 13 percent at age 25 to 54. Many choose self-employment when they retire from career jobs so they can be their own bosses and work more flexible schedules.

- Part-time work is especially common at older ages. Sixty-six percent of employed women 70 and older worked part-time in 2004, compared with 40 percent at age 62 to 64 and 28 percent at age 55 to 61. Among employed men, 56 percent 70 and older, 22 percent age 62 to 64, and 11 percent age 55 to 61 worked part-time in 2004.

- Older Americans' health has been improving steadily. Between 1982 and 2002, the share of adults 65 to 74 reporting fair or poor health fell from 34 to 23 percent, while the share 55 to 64 in fair or poor health fell from 27 to 19 percent.

- Jobs are much less physical than they used to be. In 1996, only 7 percent of jobs made strenuous physical demands on workers, down from 20 percent in 1950.

- As health improves and jobs become less physical, fewer older men claim that poor health interferes with work. Between 1971 and 2002, the share of men age 55 to 59 with health problems that limit the type or amount of work fell from 27 to 20 percent.

- Still, about 6 million men and women 55 to 64 reported work disabilities in 2002. And while physical job demands have declined, cognitive job demands and stress on the job have increased.

Despite the trend of people working longer, there are impediments that make it more difficult. One impediment is that many pension plans penalize workers who remain on the job after reaching the age of eligibility. Another is Social Security payroll taxes. As the Urban Institute notes (2006, p. 1), "like everyone else, older workers must pay Social Security payroll taxes equal to 12.4 percent of earnings (up to $94,200 in 2006), split between employers and employees. These taxes discourage employment at older ages because those with many years of work do not gain much more in Social Security benefits by remaining on the job." Consider further (Urban Institute 2006, p. 4) that

- Federal law establishes employer health insurance as the primary payer of health care costs for active workers 65 and older. Medicare becomes secondary coverage, paying only for services not covered by the employer plan that are included in the Medicare benefits package. Medicare secondary payer rules add thousands of dollars per year to the cost of employing each older worker at firms that offer health insurance, discouraging companies from retaining or hiring them.

- Tax, pension, and age discrimination laws discourage employers from establishing phased retirement programs, which allow workers to transition gradually into full retirement, reducing their hours and job responsibilities but keeping them on the payroll. Tax and pension rules forbid employers from paying traditional pension benefits to participants younger than the plan's normal retirement age who still work for them. Many workers cannot afford to reduce their hours without receiving at least part of their pensions. Some participants retire, begin collecting their pensions, and then return to work with the original employer, but these arrangements often violate at least the letter of the law. Phased retirement programs could also run afoul of age discrimination laws by favoring a select group of older workers.

Causes

Baby boomers will not go gently into that good night. Many will insist on working past traditional retirement age. Others will undergo career changes after retirement, moving into new fields. Still others will explore flexible working relationships with employers, going beyond traditional 9-to-5 job options to include virtual work, flexible hours, and flexible workplace options.

Likely Impacts

Just as the enormous numbers of the baby boom in the United States prompted the growth of education at all levels, so too is the aging of the baby boomers likely to lead to new attitudes toward aging and retirement as the generation reaches retirement age. The sheer numbers of baby boomers will ensure that they are able to carry their will politically if they are so inclined. Government policy makers will be forced to listen to the views of this huge group of voters.

What the Trend May Mean for HR Transformation

HR practitioners must take the lead in fostering new attitudes toward aging and retirement as baby boomers reach retirement age. One way is to more effectively tap retirees, exploring creative ways to rely on them rather than assuming that everyone who reaches retirement will "sail off into the sunset and fish for the next few decades."

Trend #7: Rise in the Number of Individuals and Families Without Health Insurance

According to the U.S. Census Bureau (2003, pp. 1–2):

- An estimated 15.2 percent of the population had no health insurance coverage during all of 2002, up from 14.6 percent in 2001.

- The proportion of insured children did not change in 2002, remaining at 64.8 million, or 88.4 percent of all children.

- For the second year in a row, the overall decrease in coverage was attributed to a drop in the percentage (62.6 percent to 61.3 percent) of people covered by employment-based health insurance.

- The percentage of people covered by government health insurance programs rose in 2002, from 25.3 percent to 25.7 percent, largely as the result of an increase in Medicaid coverage.

- Although Medicaid insured 14.0 million people in poverty, another million people representing 30.4 percent of those in poverty had no health insurance in 2002; this percentage was unchanged from 2001.

- Young adults (18-to-24 years old) were less likely than other age groups to have health insurance coverage, 70.4 percent in 2002. This compares with 82.3 percent for those 25-to-64 years old and 99.2 percent for those 65 and over, reflecting widespread Medicare coverage.

- While most children (67.5 percent) were covered by an employment-based or privately purchased health insurance plan in 2002, nearly 1 in 4 (23.9 percent) was covered by Medicaid.

Causes

As the cost of health care escalates well beyond annual inflation rates, more individuals and families will be priced out of the market. Rationing of health care will happen as a consequence of escalating costs that will outpace the ability of many people to pay for it or for the insurance to protect against catastrophic medical costs.

Likely Impacts

As individuals and families are affected by a lack of health insurance, it is likely that those driven to take extreme action to pay for health care will be widely publicized. Employers and government will be pressured to take action to address the problems caused by the inability of many people to afford good health care.

What the Trend May Mean for HR Transformation

HR practitioners may find themselves forced to help individuals and their families who find themselves faced with catastrophic health care costs. Organizations may be affected because health care providers may garnish wages, and government regulators may begin to require individuals to pay for their own health care. Any organized response to such issues by employers will undoubtedly require action by HR practitioners.

Trend #8: Increase in Identity Theft

The Better Business Bureau has found that most identity theft is committed by family members and not by strangers. Among the key findings of the research was that "the most frequently reported source of information used to commit fraud was a lost or stolen wallet or checkbook" (Better Business Bureau 2005). Crimes committed by computer made up just 11.6 percent of known identity fraud in 2004. A mere $551 was the average loss by a consumer when identity fraud was committed online compared to an average of $4,543 when committed offline and on paper.

Although relatively low levels of identity theft are indicated, the specter of increasing identity theft is raised by widely publicized losses of Social Security card information and other personal information. To mention but a few such incidents:

- Officials at the University of California Los Angeles alerted about 800,000 current and former students, faculty, and staff on Tuesday that their names and certain personal information were exposed after a hacker broke into a campus computer system ("Hackers Access UCLA Computer Systems" 2006).

- A computer was stolen from a Colorado state contractor who works for Affiliated Computer Services. It had data of people who have made child support payments in the state. It also holds data on up to nearly 1.4 million Coloradans newly hired to jobs anywhere in the state. The law requires employers check data on all new employees against a state database to make sure the employee isn't being sought for child support payments (Cruz 2006).

- Nineteen federal government agencies have reported breaches since January 2003, and it is not known if the individuals affected were ever notified of the data loss (House Committee on Oversight and Government Reform 2006, p. 1).

Web sites have been established merely to list the growing number of massive data breaches and to offer advice to individuals at risk of identity theft resulting from those breaches (see, for instance, www.numbrx.net). The problem is thus intensifying.

Causes

Identity theft is likely to increase because thieves are more likely to become savvy about how to take advantage of security breaches and seize the advantage of using technology more effectively than the so-called security forces to protect against theft. In short, thieves are getting smarter and more technologically savvy.

Likely Impacts

As an increase in identity theft occurs, consumers will grow smarter in how to prevent it. Governmental bodies will be pressured to provide greater support to victims. And criminals are likely to grow even savvier about sophisticated ways to carry out identity theft.

What the Trend May Mean for HR Transformation

HR practitioners may find themselves forced to help individuals who are victims of identity theft. Organizations may be affected because credit providers may garnish wages. Workers may need help from their employers to address the aftereffects of identity theft, and HR practitioners may need to provide that help.

Trend #9: Work Intensification as Employers Try to Increase Productivity with Fewer Employees

U.S. workers are working longer hours and more hours than most other nations. U.S. workers toiled an average of 1,979 hours annually, which was 49.5 weeks ("We Aren't Whining, We Do Work Too Much" 2001). That is more time than British, Canadian, Japanese, or German workers toil each year. And the situation is not likely to get better. With the threat of plant closures and offshore outsourcing, many American workers (and managers) are fearful—and will have to work harder and longer. As a result of the increased pressure, they will likely pay a price in stress-related illness and in other undesirable social side effects.

Causes

Work intensification will be fueled by global competitive pressures to increase productivity. In nations with high wages and high benefit costs, work intensification is likely to be most pronounced. Employers are simply trying to get their money's worth.

Likely Impacts

As workers feel the pressure to produce, they will feel more stress. Their calls for greater work/life balance will intensify. And stress-related illnesses, such as alcoholism and incidents of workplace violence, are likely to increase.

What the Trend May Mean for HR Transformation

HR practitioners may be tasked to help workers cope with increased pressures stemming from work intensification. HR practitioners might be asked to help monitor stress levels, track incidents of stress-related illnesses, and survey employees about work climate and ways to improve it. Many managers will turn to HR practitioners for leadership on this issue.

Trend #10: Vulnerability of Technology to Attack or Disaster

Terrorism, both real-world and virtual, is a genuine threat that has prompted many organizations to revisit and beef up their virtual risk management programs. Technology has become key to organizational productivity—and can even mean the difference between life and death in such industries as transportation, health care, and utilities. As humankind becomes more technology dependent, the stakes are higher for the vulnerability of technology to attack or disaster. As Jon Toigo (2001, p. 1) notes:

> Companies that are the most dependent upon automated systems, such as energy and telecommunications enterprises, accrue an average of nearly $3 million in losses for every hour of downtime, based on lost revenue and employee idling, according to an October 2000 Meta Group study. Information technology–dependent manufacturing companies and financial institutions suffer per-hour revenue losses of $1.5 million to $1.6 million. Health care, media, and hospitality/travel companies, less dependent upon IT infrastructure, lose between $330,000 and $636,000 of revenue per hour.

However, technology attacks have been intensifying. In 2006 "experts traced at least 1,500 attacks that briefly shut down commercial Web sites, large Internet providers and leading Internet infrastructure companies during a period of weeks. The attacks were so narrowly focused that most Internet users did not notice widespread effects" ("Internet Faces New Attacks" 2006, p. 1). Keizer (2003) indicates that phishing—the practice of sending false e-mails to consumers to lure them to reveal critical credit card or other information—jumped 400 percent over one Christmas holiday alone.

Causes

The same trend that makes identity theft more likely also tends to make technology more vulnerable to attack and to disaster. Terrorism and warfare may not be limited to soldiers, aircraft, and guns. It may also be waged by virtual means, and the capability of nations and individual terrorist groups to do that effectively is likely to increase over time.

Likely Impacts

As technology becomes more prone to attack or disaster, watch for increased incidents of worms, viruses, and other modes of computer attack that will grow more sophisticated and potentially be devastatingly effective. Individuals, corporations, and governments may all be affected by these vulnerabilities.

What the Trend May Mean for HR Transformation

Although HR practitioners may not be able to do much about threats through technology, they may be forced to become involved in the human side affecting technology. They may have to help information technology professionals monitor possible threat levels stemming from outside or even inside organizations—especially those related to stress on individuals.

Conclusion

HR transformation means more than merely changing HR. It means transforming HR to achieve a new charter, establish a new mission, or achieve new and measurable results. The trends discussed in this chapter may affect the direction of HR transformation in your organization.

Trends may have different meanings because they stem from different causes, are likely to create different impacts, and may have different meanings for your HR transformation. Use Worksheet 5-1 to help you and decision makers in your organization organize your thinking about ways to transform HR by focusing on these future trends.

TRANSFORMING HR BY FOCUSING
ON FUTURE TRENDS

Directions: Use this worksheet to guide your thinking—and that of others in your organization—about ways to transform HR by focusing on future trends. For each trend listed in the left column, answer the question in each of the other column headings. There are no right or wrong answers, although some may be better than others for specific organizational settings.

What are the trends?	What are the likely impacts of these trends in your organization?	What do the general trends mean for HR transformation in your organization?	What do the HR trends mean for HR transformation in your organization?
Rising health care costs			
Increased use of offshoring			
Threat of increased health care/medical costs on U.S. competitiveness			
Increased demand for work–life balance			
Retirement of large numbers of baby boomers			
New attitudes toward aging and retirement as baby boomers reach retirement age			
Rise in the number of individuals and families without health insurance			
Increase in identity theft			
Work intensification as employers try to increase productivity with fewer employees			
Vulnerability of technology to attack or disaster			

Source: The basic format for this activity comes from Rothwell, Prescott, and Taylor 1998a.

Part Three

Enacting a New Role of HR Leadership

6

What Is Human Resource Leadership?

In this chapter we examine HR leadership and what it means in shaping the direction of HR transformation. We will examine:

- What is HR leadership?
- How is HR leadership related to HR transformation?
- Who demonstrates HR leadership?
- What should chief people officers do?
- What are the international differences in leadership?
- What are the ethical dilemmas of leadership?

What Is HR Leadership?

In an era in which HR functional roles are constantly being redefined and in which something as generally accepted and expected as ethics is a subject for debate, the question of what is human resource leadership arises. The intent of this chapter is to clearly define the role of leadership in the human resource function. To understand this role within human resources, we must first define both leadership and human resources as separate entities. Then we will discuss how the two intertwine to lead us into understanding human resource leadership.

Defining Leadership

What is leadership? What does it mean? According to Webster's dictionary, *leadership* is the act or instance of leading. *To lead* is defined as to guide or direct, especially by going in advance. This is the dictionary definition of leadership, but is it the practical and true-to-life definition, especially for HR leadership?

To further determine what leadership is, let's take a look at what some experts have to say and use this information to derive a definition of our own that can help us answer the question *what is human resource leadership?*

According to Nigel Nicholson (2005), three main elements define the key contribution of a leader. The first element is the acceptance of the role in order to help create a powerful commitment to quality and service delivery. The second element is values. A leader infuses integrity, responsiveness, and standards into leadership. The third element is determining the leadership model. Nicholson goes on to say that leaders can come in pairs or on boards or councils, depending on which model of leadership is best suited for the company. In choosing a leader, Nicholson recommends designating a person who has the skills of communicating, team building, giving feedback, delegating, coaching, and influencing.

According to James Rowe (2006, p. 3), leadership should not be defined but should be considered a process. "Leadership might be more usefully understood as a process of organizational and individual engagement with time, culture and change that differ from management's relationships with these processes. . . . Through these engagements leadership creates organization while management maintains it." Rowe further explains that rather than simply finding leaders who can lead, organizations can in fact create leadership through organizational processes. In other words, leadership need not apply strictly to one individual or group. Leadership can be exhibited by the organization as a whole, through implementing certain leadership processes.

Ted Eleftheriou (2006) first dispels the myths of leadership in order to define it. According to Eleftheriou, one of those myths defines a leader as a person of influence. Although influence is necessary, it alone does not imply good leadership. Another myth is that a leader must have all the answers. Newly promoted individuals often interpret their positions as carrying an expectation to have all the answers and to be able to provide all the solutions. They often fear that if they are unable to handle every situation in its entirety on their own, they will be replaced. The last myth is that leaders are born, not made. This myth suggests that only a select and gifted few can assume the role of leader. The author goes on to define the chief responsibility of leadership as doing everything possible to keep employees, a company's most valuable asset, wanting to come back: "Leadership is creating a sense of community within the workplace, building trust and consistency by listening and showing empathy. Effective leaders hire and surround themselves with the best, creating a culture where people can thrive and become successful. They realize that their responsibility is to nurture and draw out the finest in people by motivating and encouraging them to take risks, praising them often, and giving credit where credit is due" (Eleftheriou 2006). Eleftheriou also defines the leader's role as clearly expressing the company's vision and helping employees to identify their roles in the big picture.

In a comprehensive review of writings on leadership, the authors found one leadership model that stands above the rest in describing the steps needed to build HR leadership in an organization. This model, created by Nick Horney (2007, p. 1) of Agility Consulting, describes the five leadership characteristics that serve well, in an overarching fashion, for the discussion in this chapter. His model describes leadership as "that special quality that enables teams and organizations to achieve extraordinary success." He states, "in today's uncertain world, the leadership challenge and the need for leadership are at all-time highs. The command and control model of management in the 80's and 90's will no longer bring success or results in today's rapidly changing and unpredictable environment." He issues "a call for AGILE organizations capable of responding to changing demands and adapting to new requirements . . . in real-time."

Horney goes on to say that "these conditions have profound implications for leadership behavior and now, more than ever, demand the skill of 'leadership agility' . . . bringing just the right skills with the right amount of 'volume' to each leadership moment. Success will only come from teams that are empowered and expected to deliver results without constant direction from the 'control center.' What this means is that leadership converts to coaching, encouraging, visioning and challenging—often new and 'uncomfortable' skills sets" (p. 2).

According to Horney, to achieve this alignment in a continuously changing environment requires the following capabilities of the agile leader:

- **Anticipate change:** Interpret the potential impact of business turbulence and trends along with the implications to the enterprise.

- **Generate confidence:** Create a culture of confidence and engagement of all associates into effective and collaborative teams.

- **Initiate action:** Provide the fuel and the systems to make things happen proactively and responsively . . . at all levels of the organization.

- **Liberate thinking:** Create the climate and conditions for fresh solutions by empowering, encouraging, and teaching others to be innovative.

- **Evaluate results:** Keeping the focus and managing the knowledge to learn and improve from actions.

Figure 6-1 shows how these aspects of leadership combine with the key processes of business to help create agile leadership. These are the leadership skills that correlate with the leadership challenge faced today by organizations, the competencies needed to guide organizations to become focused, fast, and flexible in order to compete successfully in a continuously changing world (p. 2).

With these definitions of a leader and the provided leadership model, we can determine specific qualities of leadership in HR. The authors define leadership as being of positive consequence to the organization. To be of positive consequence, a leader must take risks and embrace change. Ultimately, a leader is an active guide who makes decisions based on the good of the organization with an unyielding focus on results. By taking into consideration these definitional aspects of leadership, HR professionals will be better skilled in dealing with the complexity of transforming the HR function to deliver true value. Leadership of this nature serves as the cornerstone for beginning the rein-

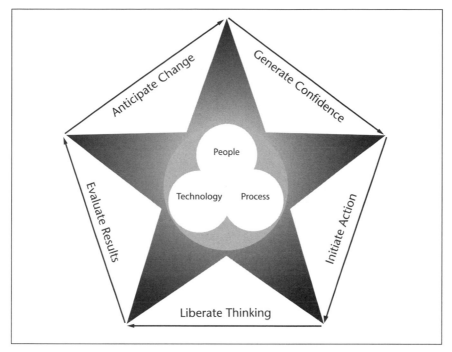

FIGURE 6-1. Agile Leadership

venting, reconceptualizing, rechartering, and repositioning of HR to this end.

What Motivates Leadership?

We have defined what leadership is, but what motivates leadership? According to Warren Bennis (2006, p. 17), leaders are optimists. "People living and working together in communities crave purpose." Leaders are persons with innate characteristics that help drive them to guide others to fulfill their purpose. Bennis conducted a five-year study of ninety leaders from both businesses and nonprofit organizations in an effort to discover common characteristics. Although both managers and leaders learn to do the right thing, and both roles are crucial, Bennis found that managers tend to be skills-oriented, while leaders focus more on character, integrity, passion, curiosity, daring, and vision.

Harkins and Swift (2006) attempt to answer the question of what motivates leaders to lead. They recognize that the question is why lead—which will have different answers for different people throughout their lives. Harkins and Swift come up with a list of seven questions that leaders can review and reflect on throughout their lives and in the course of decision-making processes to determine if they have the will to lead, if they are the right person to lead, and if they can continue to follow through in execution: "(1) Do I find meaning, purpose, and joy in what I am doing?" In order for leaders to lead others, to motivate others, and to sustain that motivation, it is important that they can first find meaning and purpose in what they are doing. "(2) Can I recite my purpose for leading in one sentence?" Clarity of purpose and being able to convey that purpose to others is important in establishing a leader's passion. "(3) Do my dream and passion excite me and others to 'go for it'?" Leaders can envision the ideals and values that sometimes others cannot. It is these ideals that help motivate leaders to inspire others. "(4) Am I doing this for me or for a cause that will make a difference?" The combination of vision and passion is what helps leaders to step forward even in the face of danger. "(5) Will I have the strength to sustain and re-create the dream?" True leaders will not falter in the face of adversity but will rise to the challenge. "(6) Do I have recovery plans to survive a downturn or disaster?" Some failures will be outside of a leader's capabilities, but a leader will learn from mistakes and move on. "(7) Am I using the lessons learned to correct course and direction?" Leadership is a choice. No one can be designated or appointed. Those who are doing so are just following a higher authority. Leaders step in to make a difference because they want to.

What we can learn from the Bennis and Harkins and Swift articles is that although leadership is not necessarily a characteristic we are born with, it is something that can be learned and achieved. Leadership is proactive. It is a process of taking calculated risks. It is change oriented. It is considerate of the culture within which it manages. It is values centered.

Defining Human Resources

According to human resource consultant Susan Heathfield (2006), the most accepted definition of human resources is "the people that staff and operate an organization . . . as contrasted with the financial and material resources of an organization. It is the organizational function that deals with the people." It certainly can be seen as a true function,

Recruitment	Training & Development	Performance Management	Compensation & Benefits	Management Development & Succession Pl.	Employee Relations & Communications	Organizational Effectiveness
Identifying Staffing Requirements	Needs Assessment	Goal Setting	Salary/Merit Plans	Individual Assessment	Employee Counseling & Coaching	Strategic HR Planning
Internal Recruiting	Training Design & Development	Performance Appraisal	Executive Compensation	Succession Analysis/ Bench Strength Pl.	Diversity Activities	Organizational Structure Design
External Recruiting	Supervisory/ Management Training Curr.	Career & Individual Development Planning	Expatriot/ International Compensation	Executive Education	Work–Life Balance Programs	Organization Development
Selection Process	Technical Training Curr.	Termination Management	Benefits (Statutory & Nonstatutory)	Executive Coaching	Progressive Disciplinary Actions	Internal Consulting
Diversity Recruiting	Training Delivery		Relocation	High-Potential Programs	Labor Relations	Cultural Alignment
Candidate Relations	Training Administration		Employee Severence/ Outplacement		Recognition Programs	
Orientation	On-the-Job Development		Retirement Planning & Pensions		Employee Commun- ications	
Assimilation						
Headcount Reporting & Control	Communication of Training/Dev. Opportunities		HRIS			

FIGURE 6-2. The Model HR Function

complete with structure and given responsibility with its multiple processes. Figure 6-2 illustrates the HR function from a comprehensive view of its structure.

Combining HR and Leadership

Recently, three senior-level jobs searches were posted through the following ad on hrsearchfirm.com: "HR Search Firm is kicking off the year with several new executive searches with 3 outstanding companies. We have been retained to manage the following searches and deliver our clients exceptional candidates. For all positions, candidates will have work experience from companies well known for best in class HR practices. Only the best and the brightest will do!"

The job specifications included for these positions serve to illustrate the needed requirements for HR professionals in current times. Read through the following job descriptions from this ad to see these requirements:

Vice President, Talent Management

This is a newly created position with an award-winning "Best Places to Work" company! The senior leader will be responsible for driving the on-boarding, assessment, and professional development process. Additionally, this position is responsible for all areas involving workforce planning, succession planning, competency-based performance management systems, organizational design systems and processes, and HR analytics.

Reporting to the top HR executive, this position will manage three direct reports (Director of Service Operations Management Development, Director of Staffing and Planning, and an HRIS professional). There are a total of 19 on the Staffing and Planning team, which will report indirectly to this position. The VP of Talent Management will work closely with the Company's Sr. Leadership Team, including the President and CEO, CFO, CAO, CIO, and the SVP of Marketing and Strategy, as well as other VP-level operations executives.

Vice President, Talent Management

This is a newly created position in which the incumbent will play an important role in the integration of all facets of Talent Development, Acquisition and Rewards. With the addition of the Vice President of Talent Management to the HR leadership team, the company is building strategic depth within the HR function and positioning the organization for continued growth. This role will support the on-going development of HR to be strategically aligned with the business and position the company as an "employer of choice."

The Vice President of Talent Management will focus primarily on designing effective systems for the development and retention of high potential and key individuals in the organization. He/she will also be involved with the recruiting and selection of candidates for executive-level positions. The Vice President of Talent Management's scope of responsibilities will include both domestic and international operations. Reporting to the Vice President of Talent Management will be the Director of Talent Acquisition, the Director of Talent Development, and the Director of Total Rewards. The ultimate objective of this Talent Management Team will be to ensure that the right people are in the right place at the right time in order to achieve the organization's business objectives.

> *Senior Director of Leadership Development*
>
> *This position has been created to work with top management to build and imple- ment the global leadership development and talent management strategy. The focus of this role will be organizational assessment and design, business process improvement, evaluation and assessment of tools for identifying high potentials, identification of programs to enhance leadership and management capabilities, as well as the integration of talent management, performance management, and change management to be more heavily focused on business accountability, results, and execution.*
>
> *The ideal candidate will have successful experience working with growth-oriented, large global companies implementing world-class leadership development pro- grams. This individual will need to be highly effective working with and coaching senior level executives and a strong leader of people.*

As can be seen from the context of these job descriptions, leadership for managing this function of business demands systemic, multiphased thinking and action. (Only the best and brightest will do!) This type of leadership requires strategic aptitude, an understanding of the life cycle position of the concern and the structural requirements that follow strategy, a focus on the operational alignment required, and the execu- tion needed to drive desired results.

How Is HR Leadership Related to HR Transformation?

For HR leadership to maximize its impact in value-added operations to the organization, it must first understand its position within the hierar- chy and its maturity level within the organization. This is best explained through Figure 6-3, the HR Impact Model.

The HR Impact Model

The HR Impact Model, designed by Robert K. Prescott of Rollins College and Cathy Lee Gibson of Cornell University, uses four basic categories of "impact maturity" to describe the functional dimensions of HR

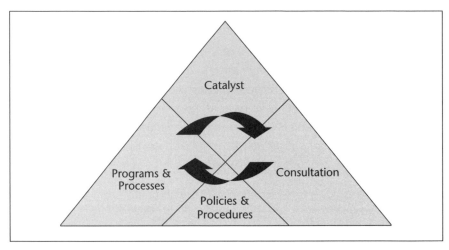

FIGURE 6-3. The HR Impact Model

Source: Robert K. Prescott and Cathy Lee Gibson, 2005.

functions. Many HR professionals operate only within the policies and programs category, which represents the traditional heritage of the HR department. Today's organizations expect more of their HR professionals, however. This Impact Model illustrates and explains the multiple roles required of today's HR function and the professionals who work within it.

Policies and Procedures

Organizational role: Creating and implementing HR policies and procedures. There is no doubt that this is an important role for the HR function. However, while perceived as policy experts, HR professionals who focus only on policies and procedures tend not to be integrally involved in their organization's strategic planning or change efforts.

Organizational impact: Influence the creation, appropriate interpretation, and implementation of organizational policy; ensure fair treatment of employees; and provide a decision-making framework.

Programs and Processes

Organizational role: Overseeing programs and processes to attract, motivate, develop, and retain employees. Traditionally, HR professionals have been regarded as "people experts" who can help build and maintain effective working relationships, motivate performance, and develop employees. Those focused on programs and processes tend to work in functional-oriented teams (for example, employee relations, compensation, or training) to support the effective execution of those processes.

Organizational impact: Promote employee satisfaction and enhance performance. Provide effective process guidelines for the organization to follow in implementing people-management practices.

Consultation

Organizational role: Responding to or identifying the needs of management and working in partnership to enhance the management team's effectiveness, both individually and collectively. In this client-oriented role, HR professionals help define the overall organizational strategy, structure, and culture as well as enhance the effectiveness of individuals within the organization. HR professionals who assume these roles within the organization improve their working relationships with their constituents and increase their credibility throughout the organization.

Organizational impact: Support, coach, develop, and challenge clients to take appropriate action on identified problems, issues, challenges, initiatives, or programs.

Catalyst

Organizational role: Focusing on the strategic needs of the organization to identify relevant trends and ensure that management is prepared to act appropriately in guiding the organization for the long term. In this role, the HR professional stays abreast of market demographics, business needs, and employee attitudes and values, as well as state-of-the-art approaches to human resource management. The HR professional points out emerging HR issues and trends both within the company and in the external market and identifies their impact on the organization and how management might best respond to them.

Organizational impact: Help position the organization for the future, especially by designing a working environment and organizational culture that meets the changing needs, preferences, and demographics of current and future employees and by helping the organization address changes in its business and operating environments.

HR professionals do not work within any one dimension in isolation. It is the unique, customized mix of services for any organization that yields the greatest impact. HR professionals have to assess the proper mix requirement for their respective organization.

Strategic Thinking and Planning

From a strategic perspective, the HR function can take a leadership role in understanding the trends affecting the business, what is causing the trends, the likely consequences of the trends on organizational operations, plans that must be developed to address the trends, and how people management practices need to be adapted to these action plans (Rothwell, Prescott, and Taylor 1998b). In essence, this Vertical Integration (VI) model serves as a strategic assessment of current people management practices to meet the ever-changing dynamics of the external marketplace. Further, the HR function can take the lead in integrating new HR components, or adapting out-of-date ones, by use of the Horizontal Integration (HI) Model. This model updates leaders in the HR

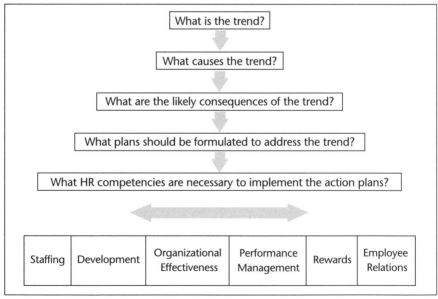

FIGURE 6-4. The Vertical Integration Model

Source: Adapted from Rothwell, Prescott, and Taylor 1998b.

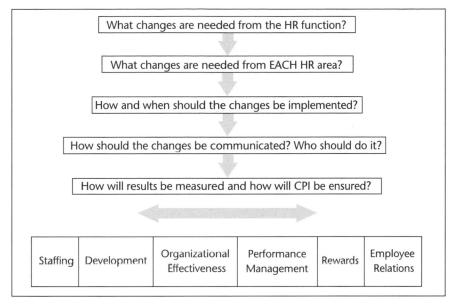

FIGURE 6-5. The Horizontal Integration Model

Source: Adapted from Rothwell, Prescott, and Taylor 1998b.

function to the efforts required to identify and focus the function's component grouping to create maximum effect. These models are shown in Figures 6-4 and 6-5 and can be used to ensure a total system assessment of the externally based dynamics affecting the organization.

Organizational Life Cycle

HR leaders must also understand the position of their function and organization in the organizational life cycle, about which much has been written. An organizational life cycle, as shown in Figure 6-6, is not unlike that of the human life cycle in that there are various phases of its life span. Any organization begins with the emergence phase—start-up endeavors such as capitalization, formulating strategy and business plans, and attaining resources—and, if initially successful, enters the growth stage. As time goes on, growth slows, and the organization enters the maturity stage. The last stage, the decline stage, begins unless the leadership of the organization sees the need for change and is able to initiate the renewal of the organization. If renewal does not occur, the

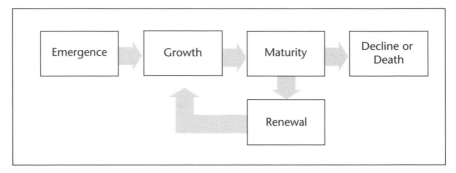

FIGURE 6-6. Organizational Life Cycle

final life cycle stage is the death of the organization. The product or service line of the organization becomes obsolete, and the company is acquired or goes out of business, not having adapted to the needs and wants of the markets it served. It becomes obvious, from a review of this process that any organization needs constantly to be in the process of assessment and reinvention of its direction.

The human resource function can play a vital role in leading this process. From acquisition of needed talent to the development of effective HR process functions, HR leadership can take the lead in asserting its role in assessing and applying and driving needed reinvention across the organizational life cycle. Therefore, understanding the position of the organization in its life cycle is an important leadership skill.

Structural Design and Leadership Expertise

The size of the business being served by an HR function is important when discussing leadership requirements. We can break down companies by size into three main categories: small (1–500 employees), medium (501–10,000 employees), and large (10,001 and more employees). In each of these categories, human resources will play a role; however, the characteristics of human resources as an entity will differ, sometimes greatly.

In the small company, there may not be a human resource department. There may be a designated person who handles the tasks of the human resource function—including the hiring process, orientation, performance appraisal, and conflict resolution—but in most cases it may be left to individual managers or to the CEO. In this environment the human resource role is loosely structured. More than likely there is an informal process of handling most HR tasks. In a smaller organization, a company may be more of a dictatorship with the founder or owner making the majority of the HR decisions.

In a medium-size business, there is probably an entity known as HR, but it is more than likely policy, company guideline, and process oriented. Its work is mostly targeted toward maintaining compliance and handing off prescribed process mandates. It shows little or no understanding of the strategic implications of the business on the HR function. In a medium-size company, the role of leadership can be enacted by the owner or the board. However, within a medium-size organization employees are more likely to be heard. Employees in this setting are at an advantage over the small company because their personal vision parallels that of the owner of the company. They are at an advantage over the large company because there are not so many people between the employee and senior leadership that it is impossible to have ideas directly forwarded to the board rather than being filtered and often misunderstood through a large chain of command.

In the large business, the human resource function tends to be more formal, with sufficient resources to serve the organization. The HR function may consist of several people or even several departments, depending on the size of the organization. The HR function tends to have a more distanced personal interaction between the department and the employee. The HR function may act more as an administrator initiating policies and procedures and ensuring the proper application of each. In this structure, conflict resolution and disciplinary actions as well as the performance appraisal process are more often left to the employee's manager. In a large organization, the owner may be more of a spokesperson or figurehead of the company, with the true leaders being the upper- to mid-level managers charged with more operational yet strategically linked decisions.

Operational Alignment

In the past, the HR function may have been simply the organizational area that dealt with hiring and firing or issuance of payroll and benefits.

But today, requirements for business operations are changing. Business no longer focuses just on the bottom line. Market conditions are in a constant state of flux, and consumer attitudes are changing. Business leaders are adopting new strategies to meet ever-shifting marketplace dynamics and consumer wants and needs. As a result, strategic HR planning, internal alignment with other business functions, and delivery of premier customer service have become imperatives for organizational success. This multifaceted perspective requires attention from both internal and external perspectives.

The HR process must have a business plan that is linked directly to the strategic business plan of the organization. To accomplish this, the HR leadership must be aware of the market needs that served as the basis for the organizational business plan. In fact, HR leadership should go beyond having a seat at this planning table by bringing to that table an assessment of the external trends that are affecting the people management practices required for the organization to be successful.

Alignment of HR practices with other functional processes within the organization is essential. People management practices cannot be out of step with other business function endeavors if this success is to be maximized. All functions within the business operation use people and work to exploit their cumulative knowledge in fulfilling their responsibility to the organization. HR leadership must be aware of what people management capabilities are required by the various business operations. They must work to deliver on their needs, consulting with each operation on implementing appropriate and timely people management practices.

Changes in attitudes about customer service increase HR responsibility in two ways: externally and internally. Externally, HR hires employees who will fulfill the needs of the company to improve and maintain the level of customer service. The functional processes required include determining job descriptions, establishing salary ranges, reviewing applicants, and orienting new employees. These may seem simple tasks. However, as the saying goes, "the pure and simple truth is rarely pure and never simple." Thus, it is the responsibility of the HR department to boost positive organizational results by placing the right employee in the appropriate position. As well, having to review with applicants the many laws regarding employee termination, unions, and contract for hire makes choosing the correct applicant more difficult than ever.

Internally, the HR function does what it can to encourage employee retention. HR helps establish employee benefits, including retirement plans, vacations and sick days, health benefits, and even educational assistance. HR serves to align the wants and needs of the employee with the wants and needs of the employer.

With the generation gap between current executives and recent graduates, HR will likely be required to take an even more proactive role in helping to bridge strategy, talent requirements, and results. The younger generation has different values and expectations from those of most current executives. Many employees in Generation Y value family time and fast-track promotions based on performance as opposed to seniority. The younger generation is also much more technologically savvy than the average current executive. The world is becoming increasingly dependent on technology, so companies will begin to rely more and more on the creativity and technological understanding possessed by Generation Y.

HR will take the role of being more understanding of the expectations of this new generation. We may find that Generation Y is more concerned with having higher salaries than health care benefits. As a company evolves, it may need to restructure its compensation system to accommodate the expectations of Generation Y. The difficult part in this restructuring is the transition. Generation gaps are usually influenced by outside factors, including art and culture, politics, and the economy. The state of these factors at a certain time helps to mold the values of a generation. For instance, a generation that went through a severe recession or depression in which there were many layoffs may value loyalty and be more apt to ensure the survival of the company to maintain employment security, whereas a generation living in an environment that is more economically prosperous will be more apt to take risks to ensure their personal gain.

HR will find its biggest difficulties in trying to introduce Generations Y's needs and wants to the baby boom generation. Most people do not embrace change. Those traits are left for leaders. So while it will be important to introduce and guide a company to embrace the values of a coming generation, there will be some resistance from the current corporate leaders. As is usually the case, in the generation gap between the baby boom and Generation Y, there is a generation in between, Generation X. The generation in between usually recognizes and embraces values from both sides, thus helping to ease the transition from one generation's values to another. So ultimately HR has and will continue to evolve from doing the payroll and hiring processes of employment to being responsible for the internal and external relations of employees, recognizing and understanding the expectations of a changing community, and embracing the resource of employees as people—not as financial assets.

In summary, in this chapter so far we have defined a leader as a guide, as someone who leads through example, embodying values that are beneficial to the community. We have defined human resources as the function of the business that aligns the needs and wants of employees with those of the employer. Therefore, we can define a leader in human resources as one who guides the human resources of an organization in embodying values in an effort to align the wants and needs of the employees with those of the employer. HR leadership is therefore demonstrated by a systemic integration of its practices in helping drive organizational results. In this effort, HR leaders work to clearly understand organizational strategy and then develop business plans for the HR function that are aligned with the strategy. Before moving into action by merely implementing standardized HR practices, effective HR leaders take stock of the capabilities of the people and processes of the organization to determine the readiness level in carrying out prescribed strategies. The next step is the development of leadership at all levels of the organization, a step essential to ensuring that specific initiatives are implemented and are backed by leaders who are effective in executing and sustaining required operational actions to yield business results. Another step is alignment of the functional processes (staffing, training, compensation, and so forth) of HR with each process within the HR function as well as with the other functions (marketing, finance, and so forth) of the business. This alignment should go beyond the implementation of generally accepted HR functional practices to include benchmarked best practices and an effort to customize these practices based on the unique strategy of the organization. Cultural norms of the organization should also be taken into consideration. Finally, an unyielding focus on results—in terms of specific HR measures and human capital impact—is required to deliver on the desired value proposition to the organization. Figure 6-7 summarizes this framework of HR leadership.

FIGURE 6-7. Framework for HR Leadership

Source: Robert K. Prescott, Maria W. Taylor, 1998, 2007.

Who Demonstrates HR Leadership?

From the multiplicity of tasks and responsibilities discussed throughout this chapter, we have seen that leadership may be exerted by anyone working within the HR function. There is a strategic leadership role—one that requires thinking in a broad perspective and that is able to view effective people practices from an external and internal point of view. There is an operational leadership role—one that focuses on the required competencies of subject matter expertise and one of relationship management in working with the various functions of the organization. In this sense, horizontal alignment of business practices with the utilization of people takes place more effectively. And there is a transactional leadership role: Even for task workers, ensuring that the right thing gets done, at the right time and for the right objective, can show leadership.

What Should Chief People Officers Do?

When HR leaders get an understanding of the comprehensiveness of the definition of leadership and think through the implications of its multiple aspects, they are more prepared to act. However, even with this knowledge, they may act in sporadic fashion, resulting in even more difficulty in driving results for the organization in a timely manner. Chief people officers and other HR leaders take a more structured approach in displaying leadership in their endeavors. This structured approach is characterized by six key elements.

Set and Communicate Strategy

- Understand and become knowledgeable about externally based trends.
- Translate trends into implications for people management practices.
- Consider the consequences of those trends for the organization.
- Determine the impact of those consequences on organizational operations.
- Clearly communicate findings through the strategic planning process.

Customize Best Practices in HR Processes

- Stay current on research and writings on HR process operation.
- Benchmark other entities for comparison purposes.
- Identify priorities for action among the organization's own processes.
- Assess gaps in HR delivery between strategic importance and general importance.
- Develop HR initiatives that are both unique and valuable to the organization.
- Continuously work on process improvement.

Align

- Consistently remain aware of strategic goals.
- Work to communicate shifts in people management practices to others.

- Conduct HR audits to measure service to other departments.
- Ensure lock-step coordination in working with others to drive strategy.
- Seek feedback and take alternative action on required changes.

Communicate and Consult

- Adopt a consultative role in implementing people practices.
- Understand the business language of others in this process.
- Develop project plans for improving people and business practices.
- Use a measurement framework for determining success.
- Conduct postproject evaluation in determining future efforts.

Take Action

- Be proactive.
- Be responsive to inquiries from other leaders in the organization.
- Act as a subject matter expert.
- Be involved in strategic, operational, and customer service endeavors.

Measure Results

- Speak the language of measures.
- Work to develop measures within the HR organization.
- Demonstrate measures in terms of human capital impact.

What Are the International Differences in Leadership?

Leadership roles can differ from country to country based on cultural norms. Some cultures favor more of a dictatorial role in the leadership of the business environment, while other cultures favor more of a democratic approach. In recognizing the cultural norm and attitude toward leadership, expanding countries can adopt and integrate new leadership practices into their own cultural norm or introduce their leadership style to this new acquisition.

According to Tony Kippenberger (2002, p. 23), "managing consultants Fons Trompenaars and Charles Hamden-Turner conducted a 15-year study on cultural diversity that explains some of the dimensions that create cultural diversity":

- **Relationships and rules:** Universalists favor rules while particularists favor relationships.

- **Group versus the individual:** Some countries prefer giving freedom to the actions and benefits of the individual while other countries are more concerned with the benefit of the community.

- **Neutral versus emotional:** Some cultures are more apt to show their emotions and others are not.

- **Specific and diffuse:** Specific cultures keep their personal and business lives separate while diffuse cultures integrate the two.

- **Status, achieved or ascribed:** Cultures differ in how status is accorded.

Leadership expert Manfred Kets de Vries identifies five cultural styles of leadership (Kippenberger 2002):

- **Consensus model:** Decision making is based on group consensus.

- **Charismatic model:** Expect a take-charge leader.

- **Technocratic model:** Very structured, provide checks and balances.

- **Political process model:** Politics greatly affects decision making.

- **Democratic centralism model:** People choose a leader who then makes decisions for the people.

In the mid-1990s the United Kingdom's Cranfield School of Management carried out a survey revealing four European leadership styles (Kippenberger 2002):

- **Inspirational:** Charismatic and future focused

- **Elitist:** Theory and debate with decisions being made from the top down

- **Consensual:** Open discussion

- **Directive:** Top-down

A leader must recognize that from a global perspective there are no incorrect leadership styles. It is important to be open-minded and to understand and respect the cultural norms and values of the various styles. Understanding the culture of another country can play a vital role in determining which leadership style is being followed. At the same time, a leader must be aware that due to many factors—including the economy, politics, and international cultural awareness—cultures do change, so the leadership style must remain flexible and open to the demands of the culture that it is supposed to be guiding.

Once an organization has decided to establish a base of operations in a foreign country or expand its current market to include foreign operations, several factors need to be taken into consideration. One is the "degree of strangeness" between the organization and the foreign country. The "degree of strangeness" can relate to anything from the language barrier to religion and other cultural differences. How "strange" a prospective country is to the given organization's cultural norm can determine the level of difficulty the organization will have in establishing operations and can help establish guidelines for necessary leadership actions. Another consideration is that of international unification or fragmentation. Other relevant environmental factors include the market and competition as well as the public and perceived behavior (Pieper 1990, p. 9).

The HR department has a critically active role in the process of transitioning an organization into a foreign country. For employees who are being transferred to the foreign country, it is imperative that they are transitioned into the foreign country by:

- Expressing expected business practices to be carried out

- Introducing them to the culture—supplying them with information regarding expected behaviors and cultural norms

- Establishing policies—setting up a guideline for recommended handling and adaptation

For people within a foreign country who are being hired on as employees, it is imperative that the human resources take the following steps to ensure a smooth transition:

- Integrate employees into the company as a whole

- Acquaint them with the company's goals and guidelines

- Assure appropriate language communication for them

- Establish a sense of belonging

- Establish incentives of motivation that are relevant to their wants and needs

Internationalization can lead to a number of problems. These include differences because of language barriers, personal and business attitudes, opinions regarding the role of leadership, distribution of management positions, and social structures between management and subordinates. Even so, many of these difficulties can be overcome. For instance, the language barrier can be overcome by hiring bilingual employees who can act as interpreters or by establishing training for a "common" language. But influencing employees' personal and business attitudes is more difficult because ethical considerations when going into a foreign country preclude establishing rules that would contradict the practices or beliefs of the native people. However, being informed as to what these common practices and beliefs are can help mitigate these problems. Establishing the role of leadership is something that can be left up to the vision of the company. Some companies prefer to do things their way, strictly using native employees as labor. Some companies find it more beneficial to adopt the leadership structure that is commonly accepted by the "non-home" country. Companies also need to take into consideration the distribution of management roles, and here legal and ethical issues must be taken into account. A company would not want discrimination issues based on cultural or language differences. Finally, there is the issue of socialization between management and subordinates. In some cultures it is frowned upon for managers to socialize with subordinates even during personal time. Some people are unwilling to accept promotions because of this prohibition, as promotions would greatly affect their personal lives. This problem can be remedied by recognizing the cultural norm and, if necessary, hiring managers from outside the organization as opposed to promoting from within (Pieper 1990).

The most important role of effective HR leadership in the integration of a company to a foreign country is that of establishing a company culture. By sending out scouts to monitor the cultural norms of a country or hiring managers from that country who can help teach the cultural norms to the executives, a company can avoid many issues or problems—including those involving religious beliefs, incentives for motivation, hiring, and employment practices—through proper policies and applications. The HR role in creating a company culture is to become familiar with what is foreign to the new organization, to integrate the practices or considerations of the host country, and to establish policies and guidelines that protect the rights and beliefs of the employees while aligning with the mission and vision of the organization.

Leadership differs internationally based on cultures and their accepted and expected behaviors. Several leadership models have been discussed that can be used for different situations. HR processes differ internationally based on cultural awareness. Laws and customs will differ from one country to the next, so human resources will need to adapt. Leadership in HR is necessary to make these adaptations.

What Are the Ethical Dilemmas of Leadership?

Many of us face ethical decisions on a regular basis, and as leaders we must epitomize moral and ethical fortitude. We have already defined a leader as someone who both embraces change and leads and guides others in a manner that is beneficial to the community. "Moral leadership begins with moral leaders. Howard Gardner says of great leaders that they embody the message they advocate; they teach, not just through words, but through actions" (Lashway 1996, p. 4). It is important to note the responsibility of a leader, especially in the business environment. Not only do leaders present guidelines of behavior for subordinates, training and molding younger generations in the ways that they conduct their practices, but they also represent the organization with which they are associated. Poor ethical decision making from leaders not only breeds more unethical decision making through encouragement and pattern following; it also presents a discouraging and sometimes false portrait of the ethical standards of the organization. Thus, a company with mostly ethically sound employees must suffer the negative implications of an unethical leader.

Most of us understand right from wrong, and in the process of decision making, we usually don't find it that difficult to decide which path to follow. However, "as defined by Rushworth Kidder, an ethical dilemma is not a choice between right and wrong, but a choice between two rights. For example, considering that a bribe would be a 'moral temptation,' deciding whether scarce resources should go to a gifted curriculum or a drop-out prevention program would constitute a dilemma" (Lashway 1996, p. 16). In instances such as these it is important to question what is the most ethically sound decision. "Some studies suggest that obligations to superiors put special pressure on ethical decision-making. For instance, Peggy Kirby and colleagues asked principals to estimate how a 'typical colleague' would respond to hypothetical dilemmas. Respondents usually indicated that colleagues would take the path of least resistance by deferring to superiors or taking refuge in official policies. Kirby and her colleagues speculate that these hypothetical colleagues actually reflect the norm" (Lashway 1996, p. 17). But this standard of behavior contradicts our very definition of a leader. As described earlier, a leader embraces change and leads and guides in a manner that is beneficial to the community. By following the path of least resistance or deferring to previous policies, one is not displaying an inclination to embrace change or leading or guiding in a manner that is beneficial to the community. The person is simply trying to keep out of trouble.

Once leaders have established an intent to lead and guide in an ethical manner, how do they check themselves to ensure that the decisions they make are for the betterment of the community—not only to ensure that the decisions they make are not solely self-benefiting but also to ensure they are not being made solely to self-preserve or refrain from raising too many questions or problems? Although there are no set guidelines to answer every ethical dilemma, there are several that moral philosophers have agreed on that can help leaders eliminate the possibilities and narrow the decision to not being the right answer but to being the "most right" answer. First, leaders should have—and be willing to act on—a definite sense of ethical standards. Second, leaders can examine dilemmas from different perspectives. One approach is to anticipate the consequences of each choice and attempt to identify who will be affected and in what ways. Another approach uses moral rules, assuming that the world would be a better place if people always followed certain widely accepted standards. Yet another approach emphasizes caring, as in "Do unto others as you would wish to be done unto you." Third, leaders can often reframe ethical dilemmas by finding a third, alternative approach. Fourth, leaders should have the habit of conscious reflection, wherever it may lead them.

Although it is important for leaders to question the ethical practices of the environment in which they are employed, it is equally important that they question the ethical intentions and results of their own actions. It seems that ethical judgment has become a diminishing process instead of a developing one. If people do not keep themselves in check, they can inadvertently slip into a state of less-than-ethical behavior by reacting to environmental stimulants, such as accepting standards that are commonly acceptable or being pressured by deadlines and superiors' acceptable practices. Truly ethical leaders make decisions for the betterment of the community based on what is right, not what is commonly accepted, and implement this standard of ethics from an innate source as opposed to being regulated by outside sources. In fact, true ethical leaders will question the practices of others and object to them when following them would infract their own ethical standards and/or beliefs.

"The University of Chicago surveyed several hundred organizations to determine which aspects of HR were most valued. When the results were tallied, it was discovered that over 70% listed integrity as the most valued aspect of HR's work in organizations" (Mackavey 2006). HR is the governor of ethical behavior and policy within a workplace. It establishes and enforces the policies and the consequences for infractions. HR is the governing body that should dictate the moral and ethical aptitude of a company. With this said, HR is facing an ever-increasing number of ethical issues.

In a survey, 58 percent of office workers acknowledge taking company property for personal use. Two-thirds of companies provide little or no ethics training for employees, according to a global poll by the International Association of Business Communicators (Norman 2006). Organizations often assume there is a naturally understood ethical standard by which all employees have inherent knowledge. However, this is not the case. Extenuating factors such as culture and experience must be taken into consideration. Without knowledge or training, an employee who comes from a culture where gift giving is a standard part of the business transaction is not likely to adapt to a company in which it is frowned upon. Similarly, newly hired employees or recently promoted employees who are solicited by vendors and are offered gifts may not recognize the organization's policy on gift receiving. The important thing to remember is that HR leadership needs to establish a clear understanding of HR policies and procedures as well as its mission statement and that HR integrates the expected behavior and practices of the employee with the mission statement.

Poor ethical behavior begins at the application process. According to a recent survey done by CareerBuilder.com, an online job site, "57% of 1,000 hiring managers reported they have caught a lie on a job applicant's resume. 92% of hiring managers say they conduct background checks on employees" (Mann 2006). An applicant who will lie on a résumé raises red flags in regard to that person's ethical standards and raises questions as to what type of behavior can be expected from that person. HR must establish practices to detect lying and to prevent individuals who lie from being further considered.

Although having rules and policies regarding behavior and work ethic may help to protect a company from legal issues, merely having rules and policies does not necessarily ensure that employees will follow this expected behavior. "Human behavior is not governed by rules and regulations. What governs human behavior is reinforcement and relationships and social and cultural norms. HR is uniquely positioned to put the issues on the table; therefore it is a critical part of HR's role to be adviser to senior management. Many boards conduct their own self-assessments and find that they are doing well" (Pomeroy 2006, p. 8).

So how can HR promote an ethical work environment? According to Chris Bart (2006), HR should take the following steps:

- **Articulate an ethics code:** HR should take the lead in creating an ethical work environment, by defining and expressing what constitutes the organization's ethical orientation. This should be a proactive approach, as responding only to a crisis will portray that the company is concerned with ethics only when there is a crisis.

- **Discuss ethics in the hiring process:** During the hiring process it should be discussed how the organization's ethics align with the applicant's personal ethics.

- **Provide information about ethics and role descriptions:** Ensure that all employees are aware of and adhere to the code of ethics.

- **Conduct ethics training and development:** Training seminars should be implemented. Not everyone will be aware of what an organization's ethical guidelines are.

- **Align the ethics code with performance management:** Most important, employees need to be shown how the part they play in the organization affects the organization as a whole.

The ethical standards that a leader has also help to define the ethical standards of an organization. Leaders who do not take ethics seriously tend to breed subordinates who do not take ethics seriously either. The HR department faces ethical dilemmas on a routine basis because many conflicts make their way to this department. Leadership in human resources means setting the ethical standards of an organization by providing an ethics code, aligning ethics with the hiring process, and providing continuing training in ethical standards and behavior.

Conclusion

Based on the research presented in this chapter, we have determined that leadership in HR guides the human resources of an organization, embodying values in an effort to align the wants and needs of the employees with those of the employer. Thus, the main leadership responsibility of HR is one of strategic planning and communication. In this role, HR is conscious of trends affecting the intended strategy of the organization. It proactively assesses such trends to determine needed changes in operations to develop or retain competitive advantage. In fulfilling this leadership role, we can measure the effectiveness of leadership in HR by obtaining feedback from all areas of an organization to determine the alignment of the function with an organization's mission, vision, operations, and customer interaction. In addition, HR professionals must work to develop new competencies and skills in carrying out such plans of action. Feedback must be sought on an individual basis as well. Leadership in HR also sets an ethical standard for the employees of an organization through establishing an ethics code, aligning ethics with the hiring process, and continuing training, as well as establishing a policy of "if you are unsure just ask." Leadership, through effective people management practices, also differs based on the host country's culture and values in international settings. Finally, leadership in HR recognizes the structure of the organization as well as its stage in the life cycle and applies that toward attaining the mission and vision of the organization with specific results.

After considering the above aspects of leadership, HR professionals are better prepared to initiate and drive transformation within the function and to deliver a meaningful value proposition to the organization.

7

Building HR Leadership in Your Organization

••

This chapter examines ways to build HR leadership in your organization. It considers such questions as these:

- What is needed to diffuse HR leadership throughout the organization?
- How can the whole HR function be involved?
- How are role perceptions of HR managed—and changed?

In Chapter 6, we examined the constant redefining of the HR function and thus the leadership requirement for transforming the function to generate maximum value for the organization. We defined both leadership and human resources. Then, we discussed how the two intertwine to guide our thinking for better understanding of human resource leadership. In this chapter, we will take a deeper look at specific actions HR professionals can take to build leadership within the function.

From previous discussions in this book, we see five essential characteristics of leadership for HR professionals to act upon:

- Being proactive
- Taking risks

- Leading change
- Being culturally aware
- Being value conscious

In the discussions that follow, we will go beyond these general leadership traits and pinpoint actions that, when taken, fulfill the requirements of the leadership definitions.

What Is Needed to Diffuse HR Leadership Throughout the Organization?

In a word, competencies! Competencies can be described as traits such as knowledge, personality, skills, abilities, and attitudes. The competencies required of HR professionals have changed over the years, depending on how the HR function was expected to work with its internal customers. In the 1990s, it became necessary for the HR function to follow more of a business orientation philosophy. By this philosophy, the HR function is charged with the responsibility of advising and counseling line managers in people-related business issues.

To perform this role successfully, HR professionals needed to become familiar with the external customers, competitors, and regulators of the businesses so they could add value to business decision-making processes from a people management perspective. This business orientation also potentially added value to the corporation as a whole by requiring higher levels of teamwork among the HR function, senior management, operating units in the field, labor unions, and external advisers (Rothwell, Prescott, and Taylor 1998b).

Too often HR professionals are uncertain what their role should be. Is that because they lack sufficient knowledge to truly understand business issues and therefore cannot identity opportunities to apply their skills for value? Do HR professionals understand their own capabilities? Do HR professionals understand the expectations of their business constituents? HR professionals, and therefore the function itself, often underestimate the power and influence that they can extend from their unique position in the organization. In this unique position, they are responsible for attracting and developing the most important asset for the organizations they serve—people. The direct responsibility of people within an organization is to perform. HR is responsible for delivering effective people management systems and has the charge to plan, implement, and sustain an environment in which people can perform. Performance is important to organizations for both short-term and long-term success. Such an important responsibility requires strong leadership. Articles cited previously in this book point to a lack of leadership in the HR function, but it does not have to be that way.

Are most HR functions prepared to exert a new style of leadership? Until now the answer has been unclear. The problem is that too many HR professionals do not possess a clear sense of what their role should be. The result is a conspiracy of failure stemming from some HR professionals who lack vision and from top executives who demand nothing more from the HR function than the (often unfortunate) role it has traditionally played (Rothwell, Prescott, and Taylor 1998b). As stated previously in this book, complaints about the HR function and about HR professionals abound in many organizations. Companies say that their most senior managers lack people skills. Even more disturbing is the fact that leaders recognize that they need help but lack the confidence in their HR departments to provide it (Pomeroy 2005b).

To overcome these complaints, HR professionals should seek to increase their business knowledge, develop leadership skills, be proactive in their efforts, understand how change occurs, and offer creative solutions to business issues faced by the organization. Thus, not only do HR leaders need to be functionally competent, but they also need to have a through understanding of what is expected of them by their internal customers—their general managers. In the next section we will get specific insight as to the expectations of HR by general managers.

The Latest HR Competency Study

The Management Skills Assessment—Human Resources (MSA—HR) questionnaire (see Appendix A) was designed in 1985 based on a unique collaboration between researchers at the University of Michigan and the Pennsylvania State University. The purpose of this instrument is to survey general managers in an attempt to identify what competencies the HR function needs to possess and what the perceived importance of each competency is. The instrument consists of forty-five specific questions (minicompetencies), classified into seven competency categories: Strategic Management Perspective, Business Perspective, Internal Consulting Skills, Human Resource Functional Competence, Human Resource Planning Perspective, Ability to Design and Implement Plans, and Management and Leadership Skills.

This instrument has been used to gather data on a mostly annual basis since 1985, with the latest round of data collection having occurred in 2007. Periodically through the years, statistical analysis has been conducted in an attempt to show the most recent competencies required of HR by general managers. Validation of the instrument was finalized in 1997 by applying principles and tests of factor analysis and multiple validity criteria to the instrument and resident data. It is considered "leading edge" when compared to "gold-standard" surveys within the arena of HR management practices. A demographic profile of study participants showed the following: average age of forty-five years; management experience of more than eight years; business experience of more than twenty years; and geographic distribution of forty-three states in the United States, forty countries, and six continents from around the world. Descriptive statistical methods were used to describe the population of the study and ratings concerning importance. The descriptive statistics presented included populations, means, and standard deviations. Analysis of variance (ANOVA) was used to determine if selected independent variables were significantly related to the dependent variables of the study.

Comparisons of the data can be made from different points in time. The authors compared findings from 1997 to the most recent findings in 2007 (see Appendix A). Of the forty-five questions in the survey, we will focus on the top ten from each period of analysis in this comparison. By doing so, we will concentrate on the most important competencies and explain shifts in rank order as to the competencies required by general managers of the HR function.

In the 1997 survey data, the following were the top ten competencies general managers required of HR professionals:

- Is committed to the success of the organization

- Is an effective listener

- Acts consistently and in a manner that instills trust

- Understands overall corporate mission

- Can manage conflict effectively
- Communicates effectively in writing and orally
- Monitors business conditions and understands measures of corporate performance
- Exhibits high standards of performance
- Understands corporate culture and its impact on strategy implementation and organizational development
- Understands contribution of education and development programs to future requirements of business

In the 2007 data the following were the top ten competencies general managers required of HR professionals:

- Is committed to the success of the organization
- Understands overall corporate mission
- Acts consistently and in a manner that instills trust
- Recruits/selects high-quality professionals
- Is up-to-date on latest in legislative/regulatory issues in HR management
- Is an effective listener
- Understands contribution of education and development programs to future requirements of business
- Develops HR plans clearly linked to mission and strategy of business unit
- Communicates effectively in writing and orally
- Works effectively with other managers outside the HR function

We will examine which competencies remained the most important and which entered the top ten as the most important perceptions of HR requirements by general managers.

The following competencies continued to be rated as the most important by general managers: is committed to the success of the organization, understands overall corporate mission, acts consistently and in a manner that instills trust, is an effective listener, communicates effectively in writing and orally, and understands the contribution of education and development programs to future requirements of business. We continue to see the need for HR leaders to think and participate strategically. Being proactive in this effort will require trust-building and listening skills. The act of understanding the overall mission and being committed to the success of the organization demonstrates a value consciousness. The development of the workforce remains essential, and this effort will require a mind-set of change as HR professionals constantly work to redefine the developmental needs of people in light of shifting trends and new knowledge. As well, the call for HR leaders to work directly with line managers in listening to their needs and helping solve problems remains important.

The following competencies entered the top ten that the general managers rated as the most important: recruits/selects high-quality professionals, is up-to-date on the latest in legislative/regulatory issues in HR management, develops HR plans clearly linked to the mission and strategy of the business unit, and works effectively with other managers outside the HR function. HR is expected to know the details of HR yet should go beyond this required expertise to drive toward value creation for the organization. Talent acquisition becomes imperative. HR professionals will need to be proactive in identifying both current and future recruitment needs for the organization. Working in a consultative fashion with line managers to proactively produce a more effective and efficient workforce to drive strategy attainment is new for HR professionals and therefore risky. Developing a fact-based proactive plan of action when working with managers outside the HR function in solving problems can yield value for the organization while avoiding unnecessary risks.

The HR function is playing an increasingly important role in organizations today. Much is being demanded of this function, and even more will be asked of it in the future. To be able to respond requires the identification of key competencies needed by HR professionals and a specific focus on those competencies most important in enhancing individual and organizational success. This HR competency research attempts to identify the importance and priority of required competencies as perceived by general managers. Examinations of these perceptions and their resulting impacts on organizational knowledge and performance have provided more meaningful definitions of leadership related to the role of HR today and in the future.

How Can the Whole HR Function Be Involved?

Now that we understand the need for certain knowledge, skills, and abilities that can be placed into action, let's focus on putting together a tool kit of thinking, planning, and action that can prove valuable to the HR leader in creating value for the organization. Strategic leadership means thinking, acting, and influencing others in ways that promote the sustainable competitive advantage of the organization (Rivenbark 2005), calling for a multifaceted approach by involving the whole HR organization. This approach involves a comprehensive and well-thought-out action-oriented plan that focuses on results while maintaining flexibility in its operational thrust. We call this the Three-A Approach.

The Three-A Approach requires that HR demonstrate leadership in three categories—assessment, action, and after-work.

Assessment

Assessment serves as the catalyst for strategic HR planning. By using an appropriate assessment model, HR leaders can understand and frame their thinking related to both external and internal business dynamics and the various levels of business execution, and they are able to target HR initiatives to yield results. Assessment involves taking both a strategic and operational view of the organization or initiative to be addressed. It involves the use of diagnostics and the identification of priorities for framing HR initiatives for action. For one consultant's experience in the use of diagnostics, see the Transformation in Action example "How Can Diagnostics Be Used in HR Transformation?"

As HR leaders prepare to assess the people management practices required for their organization, they understand that organizations are systems and that systems are a series of interdependent components. By building a knowledge base of this thinking process, these leaders learn that systems' interdependent components consist of inputs, transformation processes, and outputs, as well as outside environmental factors.

Inputs include raw materials, capital, information, and people. Transformation processes include production and service delivery mechanisms. Outputs include finished goods, services, and/or information. The outside environment includes economic, political, and social open-system dynamics. In each case, HR leaders learn to comprehend their planning and work in keeping with their knowledge of such aspects.

As each of the above-mentioned factors shifts, diminishes, or increases in its impact on the organization, HR leaders assess such changes and react accordingly by adapting the function's people management practices. Beyond knowledge of this theory of thinking, the key question is how do you know which components of current people practices need to change? The answer may reside in the use of diagnostics.

Diagnostic Models

Diagnostics are mental models that assist in framing a problem, a strategy, a plan, and the data associated with that plan, and they help to target change implementations (Falletta 2005). In essence they serve as assessment models. Diagnostic models can compel action by serving to motivate key stakeholders who are the planning or process owners of an identified need for change. The use of diagnostic models helps to reveal and explain interdependencies among system components in those targeted areas. As a change agent gathers data associated with such a change endeavor, these models serve to frame the data collection process and to organize the data that are collected. Overall, the use of diagnostic models will ensure complete assessment of an organization, a function, or an initiative. They provide a means by which HR leaders, using them effectively, can identify and focus on the creation of a required value proposition in driving change.

This value proposition can assist HR leaders in working with managers outside the HR function by providing a broad viewpoint when consulting on people management issues. The use of diagnostic tools can serve as a foundation for any proposal for change. Using these tools serves to give a more accurate appraisal of the situation, provides objectivity, and focuses on potential measures of success. Overall, it helps to demonstrate how efforts drive the bottom line.

Choosing the Right Model

Choosing the right model that fits your organizational structure or the dynamics of your initiative will enhance the potential for success of the work to be accomplished. The right model will help to better illustrate the planning process or change endeavor to stakeholders throughout

How Can Diagnostics Be Used in HR Transformation?
D. Renee Tanner, Principal, Alight Advisory Company

Renee Tanner is a principal in Alight Advisory Company, an independent organization development consultancy. Here she discusses the uses of diagnostics in HR transformation.

As the nature of HR evolves from transactional to strategic, diagnostics provide tools similar to those used in finance, sales, and production. Every function uses fact-finding research and testing processes to understand why things are going well. Based on sound investigations, leaders make recommendations for maintaining or improving the organization's performance. Finance is responsible for financial assets, sales for customer assets, and production for physical assets. HR plays a role in each of these because it is responsible for human assets, which touch every one of the others. Hiring, enabling, and developing human assets are the most strategic processes and sources of competitive advantage today, because we know people can walk out our doors and through those of our competitors at any time.

What Are Diagnostics?

Although the specific tools and methods are different, diagnosis in HR is no different from that in medicine, auto repair, or plumbing. It is the process of discovering underlying causes. HR uses methods and tools for understanding a situation so recommended solutions have high success probabilities. The methods include questionnaires, focus groups, surveys, and observations, plus reviews of artifacts and documents.

The origin of *diagnosis* is Greek, where its literal meaning is "knowing apart." When a patient complains of stomach pain, the doctor examines the separate "parts" of the problem—digestive system, diet, and so forth. Your body is a "system" with different parts that make it work. Organizations are systems too. When hypothesizing about why they are not as profitable, productive, or efficient as they could be, consultants diagnose the problem by looking at the various parts that play a role in the outcome. In diagnosing organizations as systems, they analyze the inputs, transforming processes, and outputs. Numerous models, including the Burke-Litwin Causal Model, McKinsey's 7-S Framework, and Likert's System Analysis, illustrate organizational system components and the relationships between them.

How Are Diagnostics Relevant to HR?

Especially now that human beings have replaced land, plants, and equipment as production assets, HR is an important strategic function. It acquires, enables, and maintains employees' productivity. It uses diagnostics in every strategic or tactical process, including interviewing candidates, developing training, and developing leaders.

When HR sees high turnover, low productivity, or a hostile work environment, it assesses the situation from vantage points such as physical work space; equipment; management's leadership capability; employees' knowledge, skills, and abilities; the effectiveness of work; and information flow. By knowing the desired outcomes and then reviewing the realities for achieving them, HR makes informed recommendations with a high likelihood of long-term effectiveness.

What Is Your Experience?

Tanner has employed diagnostics in numerous situations, from simple time-and-motion studies to complex cultural and performance assessments. She uses them to understand challenges and to design solutions that have the best chances of succeeding. She also uses them when designing new processes such as performance and talent management systems, because off-the-shelf solutions do not usually work. Finally, diagnostics provide incredible insight into what is going right in an organization and how to maintain that excellence. So, whether facing a challenge, implementing a new system, or protecting a competitive advantage, Tanner uses diagnostics to understand the "why" as well as to design and implement the "how."

What Successes Were Produced?

In a nonprofit with extraordinarily high turnover, management assumed the turnover was due to below-market pay practices. When better compensation failed, diagnostics found that employees left because of frustration with the organization's structure. Performance was hindered because of a lack of coordination between divisions, and career growth was stunted by a lack of mobility between them. With this understood, management explored ways to reorganize.

Another organization assumed that literature fulfillment would be more efficiently performed on the first floor of the building, instead of on the fifth floor with the others in marketing. From a time-and-motion standpoint, the change made the process more efficient. However, the unexpected outcome was diminished employee motivation. Diagnostics showed that the move resulted in the displaced staff feeling demoted and cut off from colleagues.

Having experienced limited success, one company spent hundreds of thousands of dollars on several technologies trying to keep pace with its increasing customer base. Diagnostics found that it was not the technology but the processes being automated that were at the root of the problem. After all, automating a broken process simply produces poor results faster.

Training also provides a significant opportunity for diagnostics because productivity challenges are frequently assumed to be the result of a lack of employee capability, without consideration for other influences like having the right tools, information, physical environment, or motivation.

Whether a challenge presents symptoms in logistics, technology, structure, or motivation, there are three ways to approach the problem: the easy solution, the quick one, and the right one. Each can work in the right situation. They can also work together. The quick solution can help you get to the easy solution that can buy you time for the right solution. The important thing is to use each approach deliberately, which means being fully aware of the approach's consequences and being willing to live with them.

When you fully diagnose the root causes of a situation, you can better predict what kinds of outcomes different solutions may produce. You can confidently determine whether you have a small problem or a monumental one and successfully recommend the quick fix or the million-dollar new system. Your credibility and chances for success are greatly increased when you use research to uncover the facts, then use those facts as the basis for logical recommendations.

How Did Diagnostics Aid in Transforming HR Practices to Meet the Needs of the Organization?

Every organization has a purpose, whether that purpose is profit or impact. Every action by every person in the organization drives the achievement of that purpose through production (revenue or impact) and the cost of that production (expenses). With effective diagnostics, HR uses the same types of research and reasoning to maximize human productivity the same way the sales function increases revenue and the accounting function minimizes wasteful expenses.

the organization. There are many diagnostic models to choose from, and some have proved to be more popular than others. Three of the more popular models are the McKinsey 7-S Model, the Harrison Diagnosing Individual and Group Behavior Model, and the Burke-Litwin Causal Model. The three models are shown in Figures 7-1, 7-2, and 7-3.

Framing HR Initiatives for Action

As you can see from the models presented, each provides a broad assessment of the multiple variables in working with organizational initiatives. These multiple variables relate to the external environment, mission and strategy, structure, leadership, management practices, culture, skills, motivation, and performance—to name a few. The use of these models allows a comprehensive approach for the HR leader in addressing change initiatives. In short, it allows for a framework for developing an organizational perspective, critical thinking, targeting of assessment areas, data collection efforts, goal setting, project management, and evaluation.

HR Priority Assessment

Once HR leaders have made the organizational assessments, they can prioritize their efforts by aligning the HR functional efforts with the needs of the business. To accomplish this task, they can use an assessment tool depicting the specific HR operation. Included in this prioritization instrument are descriptions of each HR operation. They then

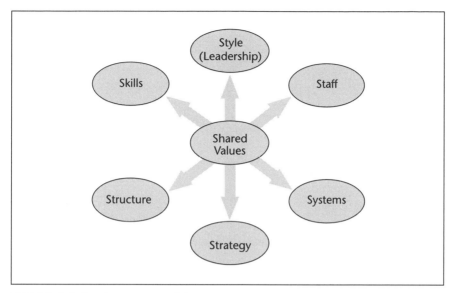

FIGURE 7-1. McKinsey 7-S Model

Source: Peters and Waterman 1982.

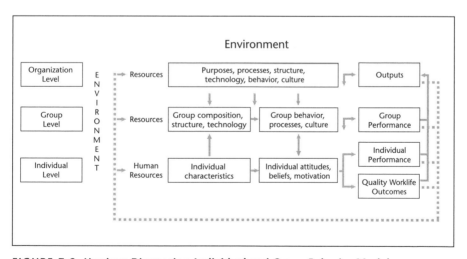

FIGURE 7-2. Harrison Diagnosing Individual and Group Behavior Model

Source: Harrison 1987.

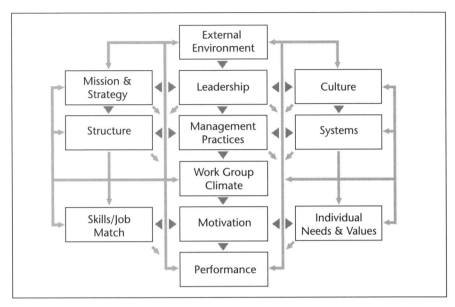

FIGURE 7-3. Burke-Litwin Causal Model

Source: Burke and Litwin 1992.

assess each operation for its importance in helping to drive organizational and HR functional goals. They take stock of each operation as to its current level of performance. Notes should be added concerning general comments about the activity and any cost effectiveness/investment requirements brought about by potential changes in the process. These might include capital costs, employee time, training requirements, and so forth. Finally, HR leaders or all employees within the function conduct gap-analysis efforts to identify priorities for action. An example of such an HR assessment is given in Appendix B.

Such a complete assessment of an organization's HR function will aid in developing and communicating an HR plan of action to better align its efforts with the organizational goals.

Action

Action involves mapping out a plan of action and proactively consulting within the organization to move well-thought-out plans forward.

Strategic Human Resource Planning

In a 2004 roundtable discussion concerning human resource management, one of the most respected senior consultants in the United States, Rick Ketterer of Mercer Delta Consulting, related a comprehensive analysis of the position of the HR function in the strategic planning process: "Strategic planning in organizations has been outpaced by the speed of change in the marketplace. This constant redefining of strategy creates a helter-skelter culture. Where is HR in this process? Is HR at the strategic planning table? Is it managing the culture? Does HR have a strategic plan of its own? Is HR the key to successful execution in the organization? Is there an HR operations plan to push forward the needed execution? Is the function proactive?"

This analysis portrays the imperative for HR to transform itself to enable it to assist in business success. One area for focus in accomplishing such a task is in the strategic planning process—not only at the organizational level but at the HR function level. As Ketterer says, too many HR functions have not interpreted organization-wide strategic plans for use in developing specific HR strategic plans. Senior executives have no consistent way to describe strategy, and 95 percent of the workforce does not understand the strategy (Kaplan and Norton 2005). If this is true at the most senior levels within the organization, HR leaders will find themselves at an even greater loss for plan development. If effective strategic planning at the most senior level is in place, HR leaders should work to ensure proper integration of the HR plan with that strategy. This task can be accomplished by use of the Vertical Integration (VI) model described in Chapter 6. In this section we discuss a comprehensive yet simple approach to building an HR planning process.

Such a plan, even at the HR function level, would consist of action plans made up of accepted strategic planning aspects. These aspects might include mission, vision, values, strategic declarations, desired results, operations plan, marketing plan, and measures/budgets. The following questions to be used at the beginning of building a strategic plan were developed, from real-world consulting efforts, by Prescott and Taylor:

- What is the historical background of our HR department?

- What is our HR vision?

- What is our HR mission statement?
- What are the HR values we demonstrate?
- What are the HR strategic imperatives for the year?
- What are the key measurements of accountability for HR in the coming year?
- How do we best communicate the HR strategy to all stakeholders?

When initiating operational plans for carrying out the stated strategy, HR leaders should engage in critical thinking to translate the organizational and HR strategic plans into HR process actions that will yield results.

Two-thirds of HR and IT organizations are not aligned with strategy (Kaplan and Norton 2005). With this finding, isn't it scary to think that the same might be said for such misalignment with all the functions of business endeavors? Therefore, specific questions to ask to ensure proper alignment might include:

- What are the objectives for each HR process?
- Do these objectives support the HR mission?
- What behavior is each objective attempting to drive?
- Are the objectives in line with current HR best practices?
- Is each process aligned with organizational strategy for maximum impact?
- What impact is each having on business results?
- Are the objectives adaptable for future scenarios?
- What might be some of those future scenarios?

Once this alignment has been accomplished, HR leaders should work to effectively communicate these plans to all stakeholders. The vast majority of executive teams spend less than one hour a month discussing strategy (Kaplan and Norton 2005). HR leaders can become proactive in this effort by using generally accepted marketing principles. The better communicated the HR plans, the greater the potential for successful implementation. Specific questions to ask in preparing to market such a plan internally might include:

- What HR products/services are currently offered?
- What process aspects need to be added? Deleted? Changed?
- What departments/levels of the organization require targeted focus?
- How will the HR services be billed?
- How will you communicate and receive feedback about the value of HR?
- What are the benefits to the client?

Much has been written in recent years about the need for HR leaders to measure the impact of people management practices on results. It is true that this work must be accomplished for HR to prove its worth in organizational settings. However, in this section, we focus our attention on the simple requirement of HR to link its budget to strategy. It has been found that 60 percent of companies do not link budgets to strategy (Kaplan and Norton 2005). However, aligning budget to organizational and departmental strategy is an essential first step in the overall measurement of impact. Some questions that could be asked in regard to this effort include:

- Does your department have an approved budget?
- Have you factored in dollar amounts for HR priorities?
- What cost controls have you instituted?
- Have the budget parameters been communicated to all members of the department?
- How will year-end results be shared with organization leadership?
- When will you begin planning for next year?

Once a plan has been drafted, the process of implementing it can begin. In the next section we look at consulting within the business. This process moves us from planning for action to specific action.

Consulting Within the Business

The past several years have seen an evolution of the HR function within organizations from being a cost center or administrative unit to being a strategic partner that contributes to the organization's bottom line. This has been accompanied by an evolution in the role of the HR professional from being a reactive employee responsible for completing assignments and implementing programs to being a proactive *internal consultant* who takes on strategic, tactical, and transformational responsibilities. Such an evolution presents challenges and opportunities to HR professionals. On the one hand, we are challenged to acquire new skills, competencies, and behavioral characteristics; on the other, we have the opportunity to increase significantly the scope of our responsibilities and our value within the organization.

Almost every competency model in recent years has pointed out the need for HR professionals to take on more of a consulting role within their organizations. Managers want and need assistance in solving people management issues. Managers produce goods and services. HR professionals understand people management practices. Thus, we have a match designed for potential success in driving business results.

Consulting is a process of thinking, not just a step-by-step structure for addressing problems, challenges, or issues. In this process, consultant and client alike are better prepared to think through the variables associated with the issue at hand. The process presented here is not intended to be a 1-2-3 or paint-by-number road map for managers to work together. It is a structured yet flexible flow of actions that serves to guide the consultant in work with clients.

A *consultant* is a person in a position who has some influence over an individual, a group, or an organization but who has no direct power to make changes or implement programs (Block 2005). For the purposes of this book, this definition will be expanded to represent the work of internal consultants—HR leaders.

Not all projects, challenges, or issues are consulting opportunities. A consulting opportunity exists when a trend, strategy, business process, or aspect of the workflow needs to be changed. An opportunity may also exist when two or more functional business processes need to combine thinking in addressing improvement strategies for enhancing productivity or efficiency. Consulting projects take into consideration business structure and responsibility as well.

For example, there are transactional consulting efforts—such as fixing a form or changing the job interview questions. There are tactical consulting efforts—such as creating a new hiring process or developing a new-hire orientation program. There are transformational consulting efforts—such as changing a corporate culture or starting up a new line of business. Consultants recognize and pay attention to the level of business operation within which they are working. In working within these various levels of business operation, an effective consultant is able to demonstrate specific skills in carrying out the work.

In a foundational work, *The Consulting Process in Action,* Lippitt and Lippitt (1986) explain in depth the seven roles of a consultant:

- Information specialist/Content expert
- Fact finder
- Trainer/Educator
- Advocate
- Joint problem solver
- Process counselor
- Objective observer

HR leaders who are acting as internal consultants should assess their skills in these areas. Acting as an information specialist/content expert means having a deep knowledge of general HR practices and/or practices related to a specific job assignment within the HR function. Being a fact finder means demonstrating attention to detail in data gathering related to issues surrounding people management practices within the organization. A trainer/educator is a person who can convey to general managers the facts, processes, or principles related to effective practices in managing people. An advocate acts in support of both employees and organizational goals. A joint problem solver works outside the HR function with general managers on important business issues involving people practices. Following a process in this endeavor is essential, however. HR internal consultants follow a process that is logical and progressive in exploring the details of any given project, issue, or challenge in their attempt to drive business results, so they become process counselors. Finally, the objective observer yields insights on perspectives related to culture, behaviors, and organizational norms that are known variables in the success or failure of any change initiative.

What is the consulting process and how is it carried out? Author Robert K. Prescott and Steve Steckler, Director of Leadership and Talent at Microsoft, worked during 2006 to review various processes used in consulting efforts in order to develop a simple yet modern process that could be used by HR internal consultants in their work with a general manager. The results of their work generated a seven-stage process of thinking, acting, and doing available to such HR leaders:

- Exploring the situation
- Gaining agreement to the project plan
- Gathering data and analyzing and identifying findings
- Developing recommendations
- Presenting the findings and recommendations
- Implementing
- Reviewing, transitioning, and evaluating the project

The first step in this process is to find out how the client views the situation. Through effective questioning and in-depth discussions, an understanding of the depth and breadth of the issue, problem, or program to be improved is developed. HR internal consultants then gather the required information/data associated with the issue and prepare a draft project plan. They meet with the client to gain agreement to the plan. They make revisions to the plan to reflect changes that are agreed to by the client. Findings for action are identified by way of this discussion, and they develop a data analysis process into specific recommendations for action. Both parties work toward the management of the implementation process in carrying out the agreed-to recommendations. The process is monitored and changes/updates to the project plan are included in milestone meetings throughout the process. After the conclusion of the project, they jointly review the project and determine process improvement aspects.

After-Work

In after-work credibility is solidified for the HR leader. After-work involves the development of true business partnership by use of follow-up activities in the constant effort to drive continuous process improvement and desired results.

Business Partnership

A business partnership indicates equality with other functions of the business. HR leaders of the future will be able to drive the people agenda of an organization, and no other functional area will want to make a people decision without involving HR, states one of this book's authors, William J. Rothwell (Rodriguez 2006). HR has a major responsibility in establishing true business partnerships with other functions. HR needs to be in the business of teaching and in the business of organization development. Assuming the role of teacher, HR leaders should work toward being passionate, creative, persistent, and open-minded. In addition, HR leaders need perspective about the organizations they serve, good organization skills, a talent for teamwork, and integrity (Pomeroy 2005a).

HR leaders recognize the need for constant follow-up. They do constant evaluation of what worked in their efforts at driving people management practices within the organization. In accomplishing this effort, HR leaders are in constant contact with senior-level and business unit managers to review their efforts. Aspects related to a strategic discussion in this effort may include:

- Did the HR leader truly understand the organization's strategic plan?
- Did the HR leader work to develop and implement an HR business plan clearly linked to the organization's strategic plan?
- What strategic planning models were used?
- Were the models selected appropriate?
- Was there an HR operational action plan developed from these plans?

In reviewing HR efforts from an operational sense, HR leaders use more detailed questions in this phase of after-work. Such detailed questions allow HR leaders to seek input from business leaders on their efforts in planning for future work. Questions related to an operational discussion in this effort may include:

- Was the HR business plan developed and communicated to all?
- Was each operational aspect of the HR function assessed for its alignment with overall company goals?

- Were priorities identified for change within certain people management practices for specific action to drive business results?

- Were efforts requiring change put in place?

- Did HR leaders work effectively with business managers in driving needed changes?

- After work was completed, was there a through review of their joint efforts? Specifically:

  - What worked?

  - What more should have been done?

  - Were quality controls followed?

  - What were the main learning points from our efforts?

  - Can these learning points be shared with and adapted for other functions within the organization?

  - How do we best institutionalize these learnings as needed?

  - What did not work?

  - Were reasons for failure clearly identified so as to avoid these actions in future efforts?

  - What should have been done differently?

  - How can actions of the future be adapted based on this hindsight?

It is this follow-up effort that provides a continuous process of refining people management practices and their impact on business results that builds credibility for the HR professional. In other words, it is an important yet often neglected step in the after-work of HR leaders in reviewing their efforts. This step is a catalyst for working to create true business partnership with those within the organization who are served by the HR process. It is also the essential process by which HR transforms itself to meet the ever-changing needs of the organization.

How Are Role Perceptions of HR Managed—and Changed?

As we have seen in this chapter, the challenges facing modern organizations create new demands for leadership (Martin and Ernst 2005). HR professionals can assume this new leadership role by practicing and diffusing the practices presented here in a proactive fashion. They accomplish this in three ways: first, by thoroughly understanding their strategic role in the organization; second, by working with managers at the operational level to establish process integration and align efforts for effective problem solving and teamwork; and, third, by keeping their sights on the front line of the organization for continuous improvement in employee training, morale, and premier customer service attributes.

In this chapter, we have seen the actions required of HR professionals to build HR leadership in their organizations. HR professionals build leadership by working to anticipate change, generate confidence throughout the organization, initiate action by use of the consulting process, liberate thinking by fostering innovation and creativity in solving problems, and evaluate results in their efforts in working with managers. By instituting the practices and applications discussed in this chapter, HR professionals can deliver on the required leadership traits mentioned throughout this book. Being proactive is a must. Risk taking must be calculated and focused. A change management attitude must be adopted and targeted at the priority needs of the organization. Finally, by utilizing the practices outlined here HR professionals demonstrate a value consciousness in acting out their role in creating organizational success.

8

Demonstrating HR Leadership in the Face of Outsourcing

Throughout this book, we have examined the megatrends of globalization, cost containment, and technology—all of which have created a global marketplace and a global market for talent. Nowhere is the combination of these trends more pronounced than in the trend toward outsourcing. To many, outsourcing is a tsunami that will sweep away the past while overtaking them and transforming HR in the process. In this chapter we will examine outsourcing with a focus on HR outsourcing, addressing these questions:

- Why do organizations outsource?
- Why do organizations outsource HR functions?
- Why do organizations outsource the entire HR function?
- What are the issues with outsourcing HR?
- What makes human resource outsourcing successful?

Using a series of surveys and expert views on outsourcing, we will discuss where outsourcing is today and where it is going. Most important, the authors will give you some practical advice on what to look for and how to manage outsourcing in your environment. They will also share insights that will give you the ability to ride the crest of the wave and use outsourcing as a valuable asset in leading human resource transformation.

Why Do Organizations Outsource?

Organizations outsource in an attempt to better align their business processes with the goals of the organization through the long-term transfer of the daily operations to an external service provider. Generally, there are three levels of outsourcing:

- Discrete Services, which are typically related to administrative requirements such as applicant sourcing or tuition reimbursement

- Total Process Outsourcing, such as benefit administration

- End-to-End Processes, where a broad range of functions is outsourced through the implementation of an integrated model

Transformation occurs through the reduction of costs and streamlining of processes, typically as a result of leveraging the business process outsourcing (BPO) partner's technology infrastructure, existing process protocols, and lower-cost workforce. In an outsourcing implementation, the BPO will:

- Automate activities that the client organization previously did manually

- Centralize activities that were previously spread across the organization

- Standardize the processes

- Provide the benefits of a technology infrastructure

- Create portals to enable self-service by employees

BPOs take advantage of their scale and negotiating powers with their vendors. They also provide deep expertise, research, and innovation in the targeted field. Drawing on their ability to automate and create replicable protocols, outsourcing providers leverage their ability to make knowledge and processes explicit, replicable, and trainable. This ability, when combined with lower salary and benefits structures gained by offshoring or using less expensive domestic labor, provide flexibility in human resource management. The ability to take advantage of working around the clock in different time zones provides flexibility in terms of time management and acceleration of deliverable schedules.

The risks of outsourcing include lack of security of customer and proprietary company information as well as loss of control of work quality and the personnel. Organizations may face the loss of operational knowledge and negative public opinion for reduction in the local workforce. In some cases, customer service and satisfaction are negatively affected in the transition (Mierau 2007).

Outsourcing allows client organizations to focus on their core capabilities and react more agilely to market changes. Client organizations receive the benefits of services by BPOs that develop core capabilities in performing the outsourced functions. One of the most important decisions a leader must make is what is core and noncore and therefore what should be considered for outsourcing.

Core activities are typically those that are central to the main product and service delivery to the customer. For American Airlines, flying airplanes is a core activity. Additionally, organizations retain as core those organizational and leadership activities such as determining strategy that create the essence of value and uniqueness for the organization. Noncore activities can be defined as routine administrative and transactional work such as payroll processing that can be easily replicated. Additional diligence should be exercised to identify and retain activities where the organization has a cost or performance advantage and where the combination of activities creates a unique value. Outsource areas where potential vendors have a particular core competency and perform the activities more effectively (Tai and Lockwood 2006, pp. 1–2).

For many, outsourcing means call centers and telemarketing from India. However, the BPO market is becoming more sophisticated. In addition to voice-based services, firms in India are providing outsourced services such as litigation support and research and analysis that involve searching through thousands of documents and complicated financial projections ("If in Doubt, Farm It Out" 2006, p. 1). Some have started to describe these more sophisticated functions as "knowledge process outsourcing." In fact, the knowledge sectors—including engineering services, R&D services, enterprise resource planning (ERP), infrastructure management, product development, and health care services such as revenue cycle management and clinical trials—are growing faster than the average (Vashista 2007).

Human resource leaders are often called upon as key participants in business process outsourcing and are especially critical when outsourcing involves knowledge processes. Human resources should be prepared to work with the business partner to provide cost-benefit analysis based on the existing human resource strategy for the processes, contribute to the business case, and help to select the right partner. Human resources has access to critical information about the current state of people costs for the process being outsourced, especially knowledge of the target population inside the organization, including number, location, salary, benefits, and estimated costs of employee separation as well as statistics on the available labor pool, education and training requirements, certification requirements, and bargaining unit involvement. Human resource professionals should adopt a perspective that includes outsourcing and contracting as an integral part of organization design and workforce planning.

Human resource leaders also play a role in creating and executing the governance process. HR is uniquely positioned to deal with issues of cultural fit with potential partners and to evaluate the provider's human resources, training and development, and talent management processes. Human resource leaders have the responsibility to create a change management and communication plan for employees affected by the outsourcing as well as to gain buy-in to any changes that affect the population at large. Human resources will often engage with the provider in implementing the changes that relate to separating employees. The degree of sensitivity and assistance afforded to separating employees will have enormous impact on the perceived success of an outsourcing arrangement. The ability to capture tacit knowledge and document processes as employees separate is also critical to the future success of the BPO. Dealing with the people issues is of paramount importance but is often underestimated during the outsourcing transaction.

Why Do Organizations Outsource HR Functions?

Human resource outsourcing is the fastest-growing segment of BPO. The ability to apply technological solutions to standardize and automate routine administrative functions frees HR professionals to assume a more strategic role. In fact, the increase in the ability to outsource requires that human resource professionals think differently about their role and about meeting the strategic business priorities of the organization with the right resources and the right potential partners. More than 90 percent of companies outsource at least one function (Tai and Lockwood 2006).

There is overwhelming consistency in the HR functions that are currently being outsourced. The outsourcing of these functions is expected to continue to grow, with upward of 80 percent of some functions to more than 90 percent of others being outsourced. For a list of the most commonly outsourced HR functions, see Table 8-1.

TABLE 8-1
Commonly Outsourced HR Functions

- Pension benefits administration

- Retirement benefits administration

- Background/criminal background checks

- Relocation administration

- Employee assistance/counseling

- Outplacement services

- Flexible spending accounts administration

- Health care benefits administration

- Temporary staffing

- Employee relocation

- Payroll administration

- Retirement planning

Source: Adapted from Tai and Lockwood 2006, Hewitt Associates 2005, and Towers Perrin 2005.

Over the next several years, the percentage of companies outsourcing the following areas is predicted to grow by 15 percent to more than 20 percent annually:

- Leave management

- Learning and development

- Payroll

- Recruiting

- Health and welfare

- Global mobility (Hewitt Associates 2005)

Why Do Organizations Outsource the Entire HR Function?

"The growth of HR outsourcing will continue to gain momentum as organizations reap the benefits, including significant cost savings, new capabilities and services for employees, and enabling HR to focus on more strategic work that is integral to the business," says Bryan Doyle, president of Hewitt Associates' HR outsourcing group. "For most organizations, HR administration is not their core area of expertise, so by turning it over to an HR expert, they can focus on critical business needs" (Miller 2005, p. 1).

Most companies have multiple vendors. The movement toward outsourcing most or all of the human resource function is based on a desire to focus on the core business, combined with the perception of better outcomes by working with a single partner. Benefits of a total outsource include:

- Access to HR expertise

- Advantages of integrated design and delivery of systems

- Cost and process efficiency

- Less confusion and a stronger story for employees

- Ease of communication and program management between the company and the vendor

- Better knowledge of a company's business strategy and culture on the part of the vendor, with the implication of better solutions

- Better support of complex initiatives

- Seamless data sharing

- Accountability

- Better cost savings (Hewitt Associates 2005, p. 4)

Often an outsourcing partner can provide a major overhaul of many systems and processes simultaneously by bringing the expertise, technology infrastructure, processes and procedures, and consulting expertise to bear en masse. The degree of change is so pronounced that the incumbent human resource staff often cannot comprehend the level of change needed. Human resource leaders must be realistic about the level of transformation required to continue to facilitate the future of the business as well as to stay abreast of information systems and technology. Astute human resource leaders have initiated the outsourcing engagements instead of fighting them and making inadequate incremental change.

What Are the Issues with Outsourcing HR?

By all accounts outsourcing is beneficial. More than 89 percent of human resource leaders and executives report satisfaction with their outsourcing engagements; 85 percent realized the desired benefits and 80 percent realized expected cost savings (Hewitt Associates 2005, p. 4). The vast majority, 88 percent, reported that the outsourcing arrangement met short-term cost savings goals, and 92 percent reported that it met long-term cost-containment goals. Fewer HR leaders reported satisfaction with improvements in service quality and the facilitation of transforming the HR function from tactical to strategic. More complex deals and those with direct employee contact tended to garner less satisfaction, especially in the early transition stages (Towers Perrin 2005).

To build a successful partnership, leaders and partners must work together to overcome human resource leaders' fears of losing control over key process, build a viable business case, and deal with employees' resistance (Hewitt Associates 2005). The degree of business acumen a human resource professional demonstrates, as well as the individual's skill in vendor management and in change management, can be a major factor in determining whether outsourcing is part of a transformational effort. If existing processes are merely being replaced by external vendors without examination of the human resource strategy goals and contribution to organizational success, transformation will not occur.

What Makes Human Resource Outsourcing Successful?

Three primary factors contribute to the transformational success of outsourcing. The first is identifying the overarching objectives for the transformation and how an outsourcing arrangement can meet those goals. The second is choosing the right partner and creating the right ongoing relationship. The third is the degree of skill exhibited by leaders and partners in facilitating organizational readiness and change management, skill which will determine organizational acceptance and performance against financial metrics.

The most successful outsourcing relationships are those where the business objectives are clear and a solid business relationship is created and sustained. We can learn from the best outsourcing practices:

- Identify broad business outcomes.
- Choose a partner based on fit, capability, and relationship growth potential.
- Recognize the magnitude of the business relationship.
- Leverage gain sharing.
- Use active governance.
- Identify a dedicated sponsor with active involvement and authority.
- Focus relentlessly on primary objectives. (Accenture 2004)

In a substantial outsourcing decision, human resource professionals have a tremendous opportunity for strategic leadership and transformation. First HR must determine what, when, and how to outsource. Then they must select a partner. Human resource leaders must carefully create an outsourcing strategy for the organization and for HR that incorporates the following elements:

- Culture
- Business environment
- Strategy
- Talent need
- Competencies and capabilities
- Capacity
- Human capital
- Innovation

Create a vision and a road map for future success. Articulate as specifically and simply as possible the desired end state in terms of the vision and business outcomes as well as culture, talents, and innovation. Identify where you are currently and the critical gaps between the desired future state, the vision, and today's reality. Identify the most important actions steps and the resources required. Outline some high-level milestones and measures of success. Use the chart in Worksheet 8-1 as a tool to start to create your road map, identifying the overarching objectives.

Conduct a visioning work session with key stakeholders. Consider using a tiered process starting with the executive level to outline the vision and desired business outcomes, validating and gathering additional input and data as you go. Keep the work sessions focused and include key stakeholders, who have influence inside the organization, who are empowered to make commitments and take action, and who bring resources to bear to solve problems. The outcomes of these work sessions are then used as input into the request for proposal, to evaluate the provider responses, and as a road map through the implementation.

An outsourcing adviser or consultant can be a valuable resource in building a realistic vision, objectives, and business case for an outsourcing relationship. Take advantage of your adviser's insights and resources to be an active participant or even leader of these types of sessions. Working with an outsourcing adviser and your organization's procurement process will bring objectivity and fact-based analysis to the vendor selection process.

	Vision	Business Outcome	Current State	Critical Gaps	Action Steps and Milestones	Resources Required	Business Outcome Measures	HR Impact Measures
WORKSHEET 8-1								
OVERARCHING OBJECTIVES								
Strategy								
Culture								
Talent Needs								
Capabilities and Competencies								
Human Capital								
Capacity								
Innovation								
Communication								
Change Management								

The capability and experience of the vendor along with the overall relationship are key components in determining the success of the HR outsourcing deal. The most important criteria are the following:

- Ability to transition on schedule and meet expected service levels
- Ability to meet the financial terms of the contract

- Ability to build a working knowledge of the client organization

- Experience in providing HR outsourcing services (Miller 2005)

When assessing providers, you must be realistic in your expectations. Look closely at your potential partner's past performance, program management, processes, and people, and determine who will really be working with your account day to day and how those people's approach fits your organization. The more complex the outsourcing, the more likely it is that you will be creating a permanent relationship. When considering a partner, you must assess how well its processes will work in your culture. Considerations include the degree of collaboration and input into decision making, communication styles and cultural fit, and "hands-on and face-to-face" versus automation.

Also do a reality check on the speed of implementation on the recommendations. The proposal must take into account the realitics of your culture. By anticipating any problems and being honest about them in the planning process, you and the partner can avoid surprises. You must be candid with your potential partner about what can be mandated versus what resistance may take time to overcome. As you review providers, project plans, and pricing, incorporate a realistic assessment of the time needed to get the required leadership support, compliance approvals, communication, and training. Many outsourcing implementations struggle in the initial stages because of the amount of time it takes for change management of the culture.

Every outsourcing partner has invested considerable resources and time to develop needs assessment, change management, implementation, and transformation processes. By all means take advantage of this expertise. At the same time, do not abdicate your leadership responsibilities to your organization. Also recognize that you have responsibilities to be a partner to your provider and guide it through the process. Be upfront and demonstrate that leadership inside your organization.

In transforming human resources from a tactical to a strategic organization, the focus of the activities moves away from the transactional. To help prepare their HR function for outsourcing, the majority of employers typically did the following:

- Defined new HR roles and responsibilities (70 percent)

- Restructured HR (62 percent)

- Developed and communicated a new HR strategy (55 percent)
- Provided training for employees in new roles (43 percent)

A majority of companies also prepared all of their employees for outsourcing by

- Creating communication campaigns (88 percent)
- Providing training for managers and employees (56 percent) (Miller 2005)

In this environment, human resource professionals must become more broad-based business thinkers. New areas of competency for HR professionals include the abilities to create a human resource strategy, to build a business case and analyze cost-benefit trade-offs of decisions, to provide consultancy and facilitation, to collaborate virtually, and to manage vendors and negotiations. Outsourcing provides the opportunity and the means for human resource leaders to transform their enterprise and the organization by refocusing their energy from the transactional to the strategic, linking human resource and talent management to business strategy.

Afterword

· ·

The future is now. HR practitioners have a bright future—if they are willing and able to take advantage of it. To transform HR, practitioners will initially need to grasp the employment laws, rules, and regulations of their nations—and keep up to date on them as they change. They will need to master the increasingly complex field of HR itself. They will also need to master the challenges faced by the organizations of which they are a part and serve their leaders with their hearts and minds, not as servants but as true leaders who understand people, human resources, and human capital far better than the average manager.

Nobody said it would be easy. But, the world is an oyster for those willing to be intrepid enough to seek out its treasure, crack that oyster, and grasp the pearls inside.

Appendix A

Research on General Managers' Opinions of HR

Appendix A reports the results of research on what general managers perceive are the most important competencies for HR practitioners. Data from this longitudinal study have been gathered from 1985 to the current year analysis in 2007. Of particular focus are the findings from 1997 and 2007 and the resultant comparison.

SAMPLE LETTER

January 2, 2008

Dear General Manager:

Topic: What do you expect from Human Resources (HR)?

We are asking over 3,000 general managers this question! The intent of this survey is to determine how HR can better meet your needs.

Business is evolving toward an environment that values people as a major source of competitive advantage. As a result, general managers are increasingly dealing with issues like employee relations, compensation, and training on the front lines of their business units. Therefore, the HR function needs to be aware of how they can best work with you to bring this to fruition.

Our survey focuses on some of the most important issues in the workplace including methods of decision making in the human resources field. To ensure that these methods meet the expectations of general managers now and in the future, we are conducting research about the perceptions of key HR competencies with the 2004 Management Skills Assessment for Human Resources (MSA-HR). Your participation can enable HR professionals to better meet and potentially exceed your expectations in creating a more effective workplace.

We ask that you complete the following 45-question survey. It outlines the general requirements of the HR function, and each question addresses two perspectives—your rating of the competency's CURRENT importance and FUTURE importance in five years. To reply, circle your level of agreement with each statement. The survey can be completed in approximately five minutes. There are three choices for your response: mail your survey to us in the enclosed postage-paid envelope, fax the survey to us at 407-646-1503, or submit the survey online at http://www.rollins.edu/execed/MSA-HR.htm.

We appreciate your participation in this research that can improve the functional relationship between general managers and HR professionals. Each manager who participates in this survey will also receive a copy of the findings upon request.

Sincerely,

Dr. Robert K. Prescott, SPHR   **Dr. Al Vicere**
Associate Professor   *Professor*
Rollins College   *The Pennsylvania State University*

Tell HR What You Think:
Perceptions of Human Resources

Record agreement level
(1 through 6) in boxes to
the right of the statements

1 Strongly Disagree
2 Disagree
3 Mildly Disagree
4 Mildly Agree
5 Agree
6 Strongly Agree

Current Importance

Importance in 5 Years

STRATEGIC MANAGEMENT COMPETENCIES

1. Understands overall corporate mission

2. Knows the key strategies for major lines of business with which he/she works

3. Understands the need to link business unit strategies with overall corporate mission and strategy

4. Monitors business conditions and understands measures of corporate performance

5. Monitors business environment to determine key business trends, threats and opportunities, and their potential human resources (HR) implications

6. Is committed to the success of the organization

BUSINESS COMPETENCIES

7. Knows how to interpret income statements, balance sheets, and other measures of financial performance

8. Develops and describes HR programs in terms of their financial implications and consequences

9. Knows which functions in firm require highest priority and is able to balance and trade off allocation of resources among those functions

10. Understands which basic technologies are employed by firm and future requirements for technological change and development

11. Knows and understands the firm's customers

12. Understands competitors and their basic strengths and weaknesses

**Tell HR What You Think:
Perceptions of Human Resources**

*Record agreement level
(1 through 6) in boxes to
the right of the statements*

1 Strongly Disagree
2 Disagree
3 Mildly Disagree
4 Mildly Agree
5 Agree
6 Strongly Agree

Current Importance

Importance in 5 Years

INTERNAL CONSULTING COMPETENCIES

13. Continually scans the organization and its environment to identify issues with HR implications

14. Develops HR plans clearly linked to mission and strategy of business unit

15. Provides creative solutions to HR needs identified by business unit and functional managers

16. Understands corporate culture and its impact on strategy implementation and organizational development

17. Serves as intermediary among business functions to help implement stated business plans

HUMAN RESOURCE FUNCTIONAL COMPETENCE

18. Is up to date on latest in legislative/regulatory issues in HR management

19. Informs others of potential impact of social/political/ economic changes affecting human resources

20. Is informed about new developments and methods in field of HR, and disseminates this information throughout the organization

21. Encourages and sponsors modern, innovative approaches to labor negotiations

22. Can design and develop incentive systems that motivate people and that are compatible with company goals

23. Understands contribution of education and development programs to future requirements of business

Tell HR What You Think:
Perceptions of Human Resources

Record agreement level
(1 through 6) in boxes to
the right of the statements

1 Strongly Disagree
2 Disagree
3 Mildly Disagree
4 Mildly Agree
5 Agree
6 Strongly Agree

Current Importance

Importance in 5 Years

HUMAN RESOURCE PLANNING COMPETENCIES

24. Anticipates human resource problems facing business unit and functional managers and proactively addresses them

25. Understands changes in business conditions and adjusts HR plans accordingly

26. Works with business unit managers to anticipate technological changes and their impact on HR selection, appraisal and development policies

27. Develops short-term plans and programs consistent with perspective of long-term objectives

28. Can assess proposed plans and programs with regard to fit with corporate culture

29. Understands the process of identifying key results areas and setting objectives to achieve those results

DESIGN AND IMPLEMENTATION COMPETENCIES

30. Analyzes costs and benefits of alternative projects and chooses among them accordingly

31. Is realistic in estimating the time needed for the implementation of HR programs

32. Prioritizes human resource problems and allocates resources accordingly

33. Can effectively "sell" solutions throughout the organization

34. Works effectively with other managers outside the HR function

35. Knows how to provide overall program control and use key milestone monitoring processes

36. Can manage a program within a budget

37. Can influence departments and individuals over whom direct authority does not exist

Tell HR What You Think:
Perceptions of Human Resources

Record agreement level
(1 through 6) in boxes to
the right of the statements

1	Strongly Disagree
2	Disagree
3	Mildly Disagree
4	Mildly Agree
5	Agree
6	Strongly Agree

Current Importance

Importance in 5 Years

MANAGEMENT AND LEADERSHIP COMPETENCIES

38. Exhibits high standards of performance

39. Is an effective listener

40. Acts consistently and in a manner which instills trust

41. Stretches subordinates to fulfill their potential

42. Recruits/selects high-quality professionals

43. Communicates effectively in writing and orally

44. Can manage conflict effectively

45. Adequately prepares successors

THANK YOU for contributing to the 2004 Management Skills Assessment for Human Resources. We appreciate your time but are even more grateful for your perceptions of human resources.

If you would like a copy of the survey results complete and return the request form below with your MSA-HR packet. Please let us know if we may be of service to you in the future.

Dr. Robert K. Prescott, SPHR   Dr. Albert A. Vicere

Yes, I would like to receive survey results. Please forward results via:

___Web Site Link ___E-mail ___Postal Service ___Fax

Optional Information

Name: E-mail/Web site: Phone: Fax:

Company: Company Title:

Address: City   State   Zip Code

Mean Ratings of Most Important Minicompetency Items—1997

Item		N	Mean	SD
6	Is committed to the success of the organization	193	5.53	.84
39	Is an effective listener	190	5.33	.83
40	Acts consistently and in a manner that instills trust	191	5.29	1.04
1	Understands overall corporate mission	193	5.27	.85
44	Can manage conflict effectively	191	5.18	.96
43	Communicates effectively in writing and orally	191	5.17	.84
4	Monitors business conditions and understands measures of corporate performance	189	5.14	1.00
38	Exhibits high standards of performance	191	5.10	.96
16	Understands corporate culture and its impact on strategy implementation and organizational development	188	5.10	.95
23	Understands contribution of education and development programs to future requirements of business	190	5.07	.82

Mean Ratings of Most Important Minicompetency Items—2007

Item		N	Mean	SD
6	Is committed to the success of the organization	108	5.5	0.75
1	Understands overall corporate mission	108	5.52	0.73
40	Acts consistently and in a manner that instills trust	108	5.49	0.83
42	Recruits/selects high-quality professionals	108	5.45	0.92
18	Is up to date on latest in legislative/regulatory issues in HR management	108	5.38	0.84
39	Is an effective listener	108	5.35	0.86
23	Understands contribution of education and development programs to future requirements of business	108	5.34	0.88
14	Develops HR plans clearly linked to mission and strategy of business unit	108	5.34	0.88
43	Communicates effectively in writing and orally	108	5.33	0.84
34	Works effectively with other managers outside the HR function	108	5.32	0.82

Source: MSA-HR Survey of General Manager Perceptions, Dr. Robert K. Prescott, SPHR, 2007.

Management Skills Assessment–Human Resources (MSA-HR)
All Questions 2007

	N	Minimum	Maximum	Mean	SD
Q1	519	2	6	65.25	.76
Q2	517	2	6	4.93	.90
Q3	518	1	6	4.81	.94
Q4	519	1	6	4.35	.96
Q5	520	1	6	4.84	.95
Q6	520	2	6	5.64	.63
Q7	518	1	6	3.56	1.10
Q8	518	1	6	4.63	.94
Q9	516	1	6	4.87	.85
Q10	517	1	6	4.45	1.01
Q11	515	1	6	4.07	1.16
Q12	513	1	6	3.88	1.12
Q13	518	2	6	5.12	.81
Q14	519	2	6	5.25	.76
Q15	518	2	6	5.23	.76
Q16	519	1	6	5.21	.80
Q17	517	1	6	4.09	1.12
Q18	519	2	6	5.22	.84
Q19	519	2	6	4.96	.90
Q20	519	1	6	4.89	.90
Q21	509	1	6	4.57	1.36
Q22	516	1	6	4.92	1.06
Q23	519	1	6	5.05	.79
Q24	518	2	6	5.16	.82
Q25	518	1	6	4.96	.83
Q26	518	1	6	4.70	.95
Q27	518	2	6	4.90	.82
Q28	518	2	6	4.89	.82
Q29	517	1	6	4.84	.88
Q30	518	1	6	4.58	1.00

	N	Minimum	Maximum	Mean	SD
Q31	518	1	6	4.83	.83
Q32	516	1	6	5.07	.81
Q33	519	1	6	5.06	.85
Q34	519	2	6	5.33	.77
Q35	512	1	6	4.62	.81
Q36	516	1	6	4.78	.94
Q37	519	1	6	4.87	.93
Q38	520	3	6	5.44	.64
Q39	520	3	6	5.52	.62
Q40	520	3	6	5.57	.63
Q41	514	1	6	4.92	1.00
Q42	515	1	6	5.32	.80
Q43	520	2	6	5.26	.73
Q44	519	1	6	5.34	.75
Q45	510	1	6	4.90	1.02

Mean Ratings of Minicompetency Items—2007

Source: MSA-HR Survey of General Manager Perceptions, Dr. Robert K. Prescott, SPHR, 2007.

HR Priority Survey Questionnaire

HR Priority Survey

The HR Priority Survey will help you first identify and/or confirm what are the most important activities within each range of the major functions of HR for you to focus on and then allow you to assess how well HR is performing in carrying out these activities. Please complete the survey using the instructions below. Read each activity, and then place your rating in the corresponding column on the survey.

1. **Importance Rating:** Rate the importance of each activity using the following scale.

    5 = Very High   4 = High   3 = Moderate   2 = Low   1 = Very Low

2. **HR Performance Rating:** For the activities that you just rated either "5 = Very High" or "4 = High," now assess HR's performance using the following scale.

    5 = Excellent   4 = Good   3 = Mediocre   2 = Poor   1 = Very Poor

3. **Comments Column:** Enter any comments or suggestions you have that will help HR improve its performance. Comment on only those activities that you judged to be important (rated a 4 or 5) and that you also judged HR's performance to be mediocre or poor (3 or below). Include comments on the cost-effectiveness of HR's activities and the current degree of investment (e.g., capital costs, employee time, training requirements, out-of-pocket expenses) that you believe would be required for improvement.

Recruitment	Training & Development	Performance Management	Compensation & Benefits	Management Development & Succession Pl.	Employee Relations & Communications	Organizational Effectiveness
Identifying Staffing Requirements	Needs Assessment	Goal Setting	Salary/Merit Plans	Individual Assessment	Employee Counseling & Coaching	Strategic HR Planning
Internal Recruiting	Training Design & Development	Performance Appraisal	Executive Compensation	Succession Analysis/ Bench Strength Pl.	Diversity Activities	Organizational Structure Design
External Recruiting	Supervisory/ Management Training Curr.	Career & Individual Development Planning	Expatriot/ International Compensation	Executive Education	Work–Life Balance Programs	Organization Development
Selection Process	Technical Training Curr.	Termination Management	Benefits (Statutory & Nonstatutory)	Executive Coaching	Progressive Disciplinary Actions	Internal Consulting
Diversity Recruiting	Training Delivery		Relocation	High-Potential Programs	Labor Relations	Cultural Alignment
Candidate Relations	Training Administration		Employee Severence/ Outplacement		Recognition Programs	
Orientation	On-the-Job Development		Retirement Planning & Pensions		Employee Commun- ications	
Assimilation	Communication of Training/Dev. Opportunities		HRIS			
Headcount Reporting & Control						

Function: **Recruitment**	Importance	Performance	Comments
Identifying Staffing Requirements: Determining the number of new and replacement positions needed and the status (full time, part time, etc.).	☐	☐	
Internal Recruiting: All activities performed in obtaining people via internal sources, including job postings, mobility pools, etc.	☐	☐	
External Recruiting: Sourcing, screening, utilizing advertising, Internet, college and professional recruiting opportunities, employee referrals, recruiters, search firms. Developing and tracking applicant pools.	☐	☐	
Selection Process: Systematic screening and interviewing, testing process. May include assessment centers, behavioral-based interviews, reference and background checking.	☐	☐	
Diversity Recruiting: Sourcing a diverse pool of top-quality talent. Establishing a presence in organizations, schools, associations who have a focus/emphasis on diversity.	☐	☐	
Candidate Relations: Providing timely and accurate feedback to candidates, building relationships with candidates, marketing the "company's story, value proposition." Providing information on benefits.	☐	☐	
Orientation: Welcoming new hires and providing information on company culture, history, vision, values, work rules, products, services, customers. Enrolling new hires into benefits, payroll, and other systems.	☐	☐	
Assimilation: Longer-term follow-up program for new hires or newly promoted employees that "soft lands" them into a new position, new responsibilities, new job, new company. Includes specific key individuals to meet, projects to complete and networking sessions. Promotes company cultural awareness. Includes feedback and can prevent derailment.	☐	☐	

Function: **Recruitment** *(continued)*	Importance	Performance	Comments
Headcount Reporting and Control: Tracking headcount against budget and staffing projections, tracking salary and other employee costs, new job requisitions, job offers, actual hires.	☐	▨	

Function: **Training and Development**	Importance	Performance	Comments
Needs Assessment: Identifying and prioritizing individual and organizational needs (development, skills, knowledge, etc.).	☐	◻	
Training Design and Development: Design, development (often includes piloting) of training programs; management of consultants. Selection of learning methods. Ensuring effectiveness of programs.	☐	◻	
Supervisory/Management Training Curriculum: Creation of a set of instructional individual training programs with learning objectives centered on improving supervisory and management skills, abilities, and effectiveness. Can include diverse number of learning approaches (classroom, distance, electronic, etc.).	☐	◻	
Technical Training Curriculum: Creation of a set of instructional training programs with learning objectives centered on improving current or future job-related technical skills and abilities (related to job knowledge, skills, technology, content or domain knowledge, etc.).	☐	◻	
Training Delivery: Delivery of functional, supervisory, management, administrative and technical training (other than executive education). Includes classroom and online training.	☐	◻	
Training Administration: Individual course/ program registration, facility preparation/ administration, training program evaluation, and records keeping.	☐	◻	
On-the-Job Development: Opportunities outside of the traditional classroom setting designed to achieve specific learning and development objectives. Can include special task force assignments, job-rotations, special projects, mentors, and external community assignments/membership.	☐	◻	

Function: **Training and Development** (continued)	Importance	Performance	Comments
Communication of Training/Development Opportunities: Publicizing training offerings, meetings with supervisors/managers to identify appropriate candidates for training.	☐	▢	

Function: **Performance Management**	Importance	Performance	Comments
Goal Setting: Process to determine and record specific individual performance targets. Can include any number of areas, such as goals, objectives, key results areas, performance measures. Goal setting is usually the first step in a performance management system. Also can be part of management by objectives approach.	☐	☐	
Performance Appraisal: Assessment of individual performance. If goal-setting process is used, assessment will be against previously stated goals. Should include both written and verbal feedback to employee. For employees with supervisory responsibility, includes feedback on their effectiveness as a people manager. Can also include identified individual performance improvement areas and development planning goals, actions, and activities. Strategies for improvement can include training, coaching, mentoring, and other on-the-job development. Should be culmination of an ongoing performance feedback process that takes place throughout the performance period.	☐	☐	
Career and Individual Development Planning: Individual competency assessment, career tracking, career pathing, career planning workshops. Completion of an individual development plan and the associated career discussions. Can be longer term in focus. Can include discussion and planning for lateral movement as well as upward movement or career change.	☐	☐	
Termination Management: A process and set of procedures meeting legal and company policy criteria that allows for the termination of an employee from the company based on poor performance or violation of other ethical, legal proprietary requirements, regulations, or policies. Termination for poor performance should be consistent with the stated performance management policy and should include a progressive discipline/warning process.	☐	☐	

Function: **Compensation and Benefits**	Importance	Performance	Comments
Salary/Merit Plans: Salary structures, salary surveys, competitive analysis, job/position evaluation, establishing salary policy including competitive positioning, merit planning, budgeting, presentations, communications, administration, etc. Can also include policies regarding salary action connected to promotion or demotion.	☐	☐	
Executive Compensation: Administration and management of salary, incentive, bonus, and stock-based plans for senior leadership/executive population. May also include plan design and management of executive perquisites.	☐	☐	
Expatriate/International Compensation: Managing international assignment policy and program, third-country nationals and expatriates. Includes salary/cost of living adjustments, tax equalization, benefits, expatriate allowances, and reimbursements.	☐	☐	
Benefits: Design and management of "health and welfare" programs. Can include medical, dental, vision, legal, employee assistance programs. Includes administration of legally mandated benefit plans (Workers Compensation, Short-Term Disability in some states), etc. Interfacing/negotiating, managing vendors, providers, outsourcers. Providing timely information on benefits and benefit changes to employees; responding to questions and inquiries.	☐	☐	
Relocation: Designing and managing programs to move employees from one company location to another, or to a client site. Can include temporary living expenses, housing allowance or home sales assistance, packing and moving of home furniture, transport of personal vehicles, per diem for food, tax gross-up. Can be for temporary or for long-term move, can be round trip or one way ("permanent").	☐	☐	

Function: **Compensation and Benefits** (continued)	Importance	Performance	Comments
Employee Severance/Outplacement: Managing downsizing, severance, and outplacement. May include internal or external career transition programs, resume writing, and interviewing skills workshops.	☐	▨	
Retirement Planning and Pensions: Designing and managing retirement planning process and programs. Can include pre-retirement planning and workshops, company pension plans, 401(k) plans, company matching formulas. Includes vendor selection and management. Timely communication to employees of current plans and programs and any changes.	☐	▨	
HRIS: All activities related to employee information collection, analysis and reporting, including automated and computerized systems. May include workforce information, payroll, and benefits information. Selection and management of vendors and consultants.	☐	▨	

Function: **Management Development and Succession Planning**	Importance	Performance	Comments
Individual Assessment: Assessment using systematic process of individual's current effectiveness and/or future advancement potential or promotability. May include behavioral-based interviewing, assessment center approach, testing, etc. Can include identification of strengths and needed improvement areas. May include assessment of what it will take to retain a key individual.	☐	☐	
Succession Analysis/Bench Strength Planning: Developing plans for the orderly replacement/staffing of key positions and/or senior levels of management. Includes identifying, developing, and placing high-potential individuals; coordinating cross-functional assignments; and creating and maintaining a database of individuals who are within the "plan." Can include identification of gaps; positions where openings will have to be filled via external recruiting. Organizational view of current management strength, near-term replacements, and identified actions needed.	☐	☐	
Executive Education: Programs that focus on developing executives for current and/or future challenges as leaders and managers. Can include internal developed and presented programs, university-designed public programs or customized programs. Usually multiday in length and often include recognized leaders/experts from consulting companies, academia, executives from other companies to speak on business and/or leadership related topics. Programs often include use of 360 feedback with executive coaching.	☐	☐	
Executive Coaching: Use of either an internal or external coach assigned to an executive to focus on increasing executive effectiveness in a specific area (communications, managing subordinates, executing strategy). Should include clear developmental objectives, measurement criteria, clarity around issues of confidentiality, duration of coaching relationship.	☐	☐	

Function: **Management Development** and **Succession Planning** *(continued)*	Importance	Performance	Comments
High-Potential Programs: Identification of current employees who have either significant advancement potential or future promotability, usually to key positions or senior levels of management. Includes identifying these individuals and creating and managing special development plans and programs. Development activities often include special classroom programs, mentoring, coaching, rotations, task force leadership or membership, directed placements, 360 feedback.	☐	☐	

Function: **Employee Relations and Communications**	Importance	Performance	Comments
Employee Counseling and Coaching: Responding to employee questions and concerns in the appropriate manner. Resolving issues between employees and supervisors. Can include referral to employee assistance service.	☐	☐	
Diversity Activities: Programs aimed at encouraging and developing a diverse workforce and management team in terms of race, religion, gender, sexual orientation, and physical limitations/challenges. Often presented as part of business case; diversity of customers and benefits of having diverse employees who can bring in varied perspectives to solve business challenges.	☐	☐	
Work–Life Balance Programs: Programs, policies, activities related to managing work and family life issues. May include fitness programs, on-site child care, elder care, flexible work schedules, job sharing, and telecommuting.	☐	☐	
Progressive Disciplinary Actions: Policies and actions that are related to disciplinary procedures and processes. Written policies, which usually include graduated escalating steps and sanctions.	☐	☐	
Labor Relations: Plans in place for proactive labor negotiations including assessments of labor demands and tactics to address each. Advance planning and labor negotiation team identified.	☐	☐	
Recognition Programs: Programs that recognize and appreciate employees via nonmonetary rewards/awards. Can include company service awards, perfect attendance record, and individual and team accomplishment recognition.	☐	☐	

Function: **Employee Relations and** **Communications** (continued)	Importance	Performance	Comments
Employee Communications: Planned communications to employees on business results, leadership changes, acquisitions, structural changes, benefit changes, etc. Can include paper newsletters, company Web postings/broadcasts, e-mails, broadcast voicemails, town hall meetings. Sometimes are two-way in nature and may include focus groups, "skip-level" sessions, etc.	☐	☐	

Function: **Organizational Effectiveness**	Importance	Performance	Comments
Strategic HR Planning: Proactively linking HR plans to business strategy and objectives, including prioritization and resource allocation for HR programs to maximize impact and return for business. Usually includes identifying HR issues/implications/challenges created by business strategies/objectives and then having a well-thought-out HR response.	☐	▢	
Organizational Structure Design: Creating the organization's structure (reporting relationships, span of control, levels of management, groupings of units and numbers of employees) to most effectively support the achievement of desired business objectives and performance. Usually represented by organization charts (lines and boxes) with various information on the chart. Factors in where the planning, leading, and doing should be done.	☐	▢	
Organization Development: The key work processes necessary to successfully carry out all stages of the work from design to customer sales/delivery and the developmental requirements for each step.	☐	▢	
Internal Consulting: HR professionals trained and assigned to work proactively with line managers in addressing people management issues in line units.	☐	▢	
Cultural Alignment: Assessing the culture against the business goals and objectives and then if necessary strengthening the alignment. For example: Is the culture very adverse to risk taking while the business strategy calls for bolder moves and more risky decisions? Includes looking at company hiring, promotion, reward and recognition programs, and required leadership and employee behavior.	☐	▢	

References

....

Accenture. 2004. *Driving High Performance Consulting: Best Practices from the Masters, Executive Survey Results.* http://www.accenture.com/Global/ Research_ and_Insights/By_Subject/Business_Process_Outsourcing/Accenture_HR_Services/ DrivingMasters.htm.

Adams, M. 2005. "Health Insurance Coverage No. 1 Problem Facing U.S. Employers, Says Penn State Professor." NewsTarget.com. http://www.newstarget.com/ z008331.html (accessed December 29, 2006).

Amazon.com, Inc. 2006. "Amazon.com Announces Third Quarter Financial Results—Net Sales Up 24% Year Over Year—Expects Record Holiday Season." Press release, October 24. http://www.phk.corporate-ir.net/phoenix.zhtml?c= 97664ap=irol-newsarticle@ID=920528@highlights.

Anderson, D. M. 2007. "Design for Manufacturability." Design for Manufactur-ability. http://www.design4manufacturability.com/DFM_article.htm.

Armstrong-Stassen, M. 2006. "Encouraging Retirees to Return to the Workforce." *Human Resource Planning* 29, no. 4: 38–44.

Bart, C. 2006. "Promoting an Ethical Work Environment." *Canadian HR Reporter* 19, no. 18 (October 23): 25–26.

Bennis, W. 2006. "Why Lead?" *Leadership Excellence* 23, no. 10 (October): 4–5.

Better Business Bureau. 2005. "New Research Shows That Identity Theft Is More Prevalent Offline with Paper than Online." http://www.bbb.org/alerts/article. asp?ID=565 (accessed December 24, 2006).

Block, P. 2000. *Flawless Consulting: A Guide to Getting Your Expertise Used.* San Francisco: Jossey-Bass/Pfeiffer.

Brecker, S., R. Prescott, and S. Steckler. 2006. "Internal Consulting Skills." Unpublished manuscript, New York.

Burke, W., and A. Litwin. 1992. "A Casual Model of Organizational Performance and Change." *Journal of Management* 18, no. 3: 523–545.

Capital One Financial Corporation. 2007. "Capital One Named One of Fortune Magazine's 100 Best Companies to Work For." News release, January 8. http://www.capitalone.com/.

CarMax. 2007. "CarMax Named One of the '100 Best Companies to Work For' by Fortune Magazine for the Third Year in a Row." Press release, January 8. http://media.carmax.com/pr/carmax/info/100Best2007.asp.

Cauchon, D., and J. Waggoner. 2004. "The Looming National Benefit Crisis." *USA Today,* October 3. http://www.usatoday.com/news/nation/2004-10-03-debt-cover_x.htm (accessed February 1, 2008).

Caudron, S. 2005. "HR Is Dead, Long Live HR." *Workforce,* January, pp. 26–30.

Center for Applied Research. 1999. "Campaign Approach to Organizational Change." Briefing Notes: Center for Applied Research.

Christensen, R. 2005. *Roadmap to Strategic HR: Turning a Great Idea Into a Business Reality.* New York: Amacom.

Christoffersen, J. 2007. "In a Changing World, GE Spreads Globally." *U.S. News & World Report,* January 14. http://www.USNews.com/.

Clarke, T. President, General Motors North America. 2006a. "Gaining Momentum in the GMNA Turnaround: Next Steps." Speech, November 21. http://media.gm.com:8221/servlet/GatewayServlet?target=http://image.emerald.gm.com/gmnews/viewmediaspeechdetail.do?domain=588&docid=30654 (accessed February 1, 2008).

———. 2006b. "Continuing Momentum: In GM and in Lansing." Speech, December 7. http://media.gm.com:8221/servlet/GatewayServlet?target=http://image.emerald.gm.com/gmnews/viewmediaspeechdetail.do?domain=588&docid=31184 (accessed February 1, 2008).

Claus, L., and J. Collison. 2004. *SHRM/SHRM Global Forum's The Maturing Profession of Human Resources in the United States of America Survey Report.* Arlington, VA: Society for Human Resource Management.

Collis, D., and C. Montgomery. 1998. *Corporate Strategy: A Resource-Based Approach.* Boston: McGraw-Hill.

Columbia, K. 2005. "Addressing Generational Diversity." *Newspapers & Technology,* October. http://www.newsandtech.com/issues/10–05/nt/10-05_columbia.htm.

Cruz, M. 2006. "1.4 Million Coloradans at Risk to Identity Theft." NumberX Security Beat. http://www.numbrx.net/2006/11/02/14-million-coloradans-at-risk-to-identity-theft/.

Cummings, Jeffrey L., Beng-Sheng Teng, Stephen C. Heilman, Darrell P. Ahne. 2002. "Do You Really Know Your Capabilities? A Dynamic Internal Analysis." November 14, Department of Management and International Business, Sellinger School of Business and Management, Loyola College in Maryland.

Davis, I., and E. Stephenson. 2006. "Ten Trends to Watch in 2006." *McKinsey Quarterly,* Web exclusive, January, pp. 1–6. http://www.mckinseyquarterly.com/links/22698.

Deutsch, C. H. 2005. "Gillette Balances Goals an a New Razor's Edge." *International Herald Tribune,* September 15. http://www.iht.com.

Dohm, A. 2000. "Gauging the Labor Force Effects of Retiring Baby-Boomers." *Monthly Labor Review Online* 123, no. 7. http://www.bls.gov/opub/mlr/2000/07/art2exc.htm (accessed December 23, 2006.

Drucker, P. 1954. *The Practice of Management.* New York: Harper.

Drucker, P., et al. 1997. "Looking Ahead: Implications of the Present: The Future Has Already Happened." *Harvard Business Review,* September–October, pp. 20–24.

Eleftheriou, T. 2006. "Playbook: Defining Leadership." *Parks and Recreation,* 41, no. 11 (November): 20–21.

Engardio, P., D. Roberts, and B. Bremner. 2004. "The China Price." *Business Week,* December 6. http://www.businessweek.com/magazine/toc/04_49/B39110449china.htm.

Evans, P. B., and T. S. Wurster. 1997. "Strategy and the New Economies of Information." *Harvard Business Review,* September–October 1997, pp. 70–82.

"Everybody's Doing It: Companies of All Stripes Have Become Aware of the Need to Gather Talent." 2006. *Economist,* October 5, pp. 1–4. http://www.economist.com/.

"An Executive Take on the Top Business Trends: A McKinsey Global Survey." 2006. *McKinsey Quarterly,* Web exclusive, April, pp. 1–5. http://www.mckinseyquarterly.com/links/2269.

Falletta, S. V. 2005. "Organizational Diagnostic Models: A Review and Synthesis." White paper. Sunnyvale, CA.

Fischer, K. 2003. "Transforming HR Globally: The Center of Excellence Approach." *Human Resource Planning* 75, no. 2: 9.

Frey, W. 1999. "The United States Population: Where the New Immigrants Are." *U.S. Society and Values,* Electronic Journal of the U.S. Information Agency 4, no. 2 (June). http://www.usinfo.state.gov/journals/itsv/0699/ijse/toc.htm.

Galbraith, J. *Designing Organizations: An Executive Guide to Strategy, Structure, and Process.* 2001. San Francisco: Jossey-Bass.

Garvin, G. A., and L. C. Levesque. 2006. "Meeting the Challenge of Corporate Entrepreneurship." *Harvard Business Review* 84, no. 10 (October): 102–112.

Giancola, F. 2006. "The Generation Gap: More Myth than Reality." *Human Resource Planning,* 29, no. 4: 32–37.

"Global Survey of Business Executives." 2006. *McKinsey Quarterly,* March.

Greemore, S. 2005. "Human Capital Strategic Plan Receives High Marks from DoD and Sets DCMA's Transformation Roadmap." Defense Contract Management Agency. http://www.dcma.mil/.

Gutierrez, C. 2006. "Remarks to the American Chamber of Commerce, Sao Paulo, Brazil." Remarks by U.S. Commerce Secretary Carlos Gutierrez, June 8. http://www.commerce.gov/.

"Hackers Access UCLA Computer Systems." 2006. CBS News, December 12. http://www.cbsnews.com/stories/2006/12/12/tech/main2249716.shtml (accessed December 24, 2006).

Hamm, S. 2006. "Big Blue Shift." *Business Week,* June 5, pp. 108–110.

Hammonds, K. 2005. "Why We Hate HR." *Fast Company,* August, p. 40.

Harkins, P., and P. Swift. 2006. "Seven Leadership Principles." *Leadership Excellence* 23, no. 5 (May): 7.

Harrison, M. I. 1987. *Diagnosing Organizations: Methods, Models, and Processes.* Newbury Park, CA: Sage.

Heathfield, S. 2006. "What is the Definition of Human Resources?" About.com: Human Resources. http://humanresources.about.com/od/glossary (accessed December 21, 2006).

Henkoff, R. 1997. "The Fortune Five-Hundred: A Year of Extraordinary Gains." *Fortune,* April 28, pp. 193–197.

Hewitt Associates. 2005. *Survey Highlights HR Outsourcings: Trends and Insights 2005.* http://www.hewittassociates.com/articles/hrtrends_highlights.pdf.

Hirshhorn, L. 2002. "Campaigning for Change." *Harvard Business Review,* July, pp. 98–104.

Horney, N. 2007 "Agile Leadership Conseling." http://www.agilityconsulting.com/services/AgileLeadershipCoaching.pdf.

House Committee on Oversight and Government Reform. 2006. *Report: Data Held by Federal Agencies Remains at Risk.* http://reform.house.gov/UploadedFiles/Agency%20Breach%20Summary%20Final%20(3).pdf (accessed December 24, 2006).

Howe, N., and W. Straus. 2000. *Millennials Rising: The Next Great Generation.* New York: Vintage Books.

"'If in Doubt, Farm It Out'; Survey: Business in India." 2006. *Economist,* June 1, pp. 1–4, *www.economist.com/.*

"India on Fire." 2007. *Economist,* February 3, pp. 69–71.

"India: Surf Excel Relaunched to Reduce Rinsing and Conserve Water." Unilever. http://www.unilever.com/ourbrands/homecare/Surf.asp.

"Internet Faces New Attacks." 2006. *International Herald Tribune,* March 16, 2006. http://www.iht.com/articles/2006/03/16/business/net.php (accessed December 29, 2006).

Johnson, J. 1997. "Address to the U.S. Naval Institute," Annapolis, MD, April 23. http://www.navy.mil/navydata/people/flags/Johnson-j/speeches/usn10423.txt.

Jones, C. 2003. "Why Have Health Expenditures as a Share of GDP Risen So Much?" Paper presented at the annual meeting of the American Public Health Association, November 17. http://apha.confex.com/apha/131am/techprogram/paper_74235.htm (accessed December 23, 2006).

Jones, D. 2007. "Toyota's Success Pleases Proponents of 'Lean.'" *USA Today,* May 3, 2B.

Kaplan, R., and D. Norton. 2005. "The Office of Strategy Management." *Harvard Business Review,* October.

Keizer, G. 2003. "Phishing Attacks Soar." *TechWeb,* December 24. http://www.tech web.com/wire/story/TWB20031224S0006 (accessed December 23, 2006).

Kelley, T., and J. Littman. 2005. *Ten Faces of Innovation: IDEO's Strategies for Beating the Devil's Advocate and Driving Creativity Throughout Your Organization.* New York: Doubleday.

Kippenberger, T. 2002. *Leadership Styles*. Oxford, U.K.: Capstone.

Lashway, L. 1996. "Ethical Leadership." *Clearinghouse on Educational Policy and Management,* June. http://eric.uoregon.edu/publications/digests (accessed December 25, 2006).

Lawler, E., D. Ulrich, J. Fitz-Enz, J. Madden, and R. Maruca. 2004. *Human Resources Business Process Outsourcing: Transforming How HR Gets Its Work Done.* San Francisco: Jossey-Bass.

Lawler, E., J. Boudreau, and S. Mohrman. 2006. *Achieving Strategic Excellence: An Assessment of Human Resource Organizations.* With A. Mark, B. Neilson, and N. Osganian. Stanford, CA: Stanford Business Books.

Lippitt, G., and R. Lippitt. 1986. *The Consulting Process in Action.* San Diego: Pfeiffer.

Litwin, G., and R. Stringer. 1968. *Organizational Climate Questionnaire.* Graduate School of Business Administration, Harvard University, Cambridge, MA.

Mackavey, M. 2006. "Practicing Ethics in HR: Where's the Action?" *Journal of American Academy of Business* 9, no. 2 (September): 244–250.

Mann, J. 2006. "Lie on Resume at Own Risk." *Knight Ridder Tribune Business News,* October 30, p. 1.

"Manpower: The World of Work." 2007. *Economist,* January 4. http://www.economist.com/business/displaystory.cfm?story_id=8486118.

Martin, A., and C. Ernst. 2005. "Leadership, Learning, and Human Resource Management: Exploring Leadership in Times of Paradox and Complexity." *Corporate Governance* 5, no. 3: 82–95.

"Masters of the Universe." 2006. *Economist,* October 5. http://www.economist.com/surveys/displaystory.cfm?story_id=7961906.

McGirt, E. 2006. "A Banner Year: Despite a World of Trouble, the 500—Led by Banking, Oil, Drugs, and Insurance—Roared Ahead." *Fortune,* April 17, pp. 192–195.

Mierau, A. 2007. "Strategic Importance of Knowledge Process Outsourcing," Technical University of Kaiserslautern, Germany.

Miller, S. 2005a. "Organizations That Outsource HR Seek Standardization, Ability to Focus on Business Issues." http://www.shrm.org/outsourcing/ news_published/ CMS_019505.asp (accessed December 29, 2006).

———. 2005b. "Survey: 'Losing Control' Is Clients' Top HR Outsourcing Fear." *SHRM HR Outsourcing Forum,* Society for Human Resource Management, April 2005. http://www.shrm.org/outsourcing.

"Nearly $3 Trillion Dollars in U.S. Health Spending Is Projected." 2002. Mercola.com. http://www.mercola.com/2002/mar/30/health_spending.htm (accessed December 21, 2006). Reprinted from *Health Affairs* 21 (March/April 2002): 207–217.

Nicholson, N. 2005. "What, Who and How." *Leadership Excellence* 22, no. 3 (March): 15.

"Nightmare Scenarios: Western Worries About Losing Job and Talents Are Only Partly Justified." 2006. *Economist,* October 5. http://www.economist.com/surveys/displaystory.cfm?story_id=7961926.

Norman, J. 2006. "Cultivating a Culture of Honesty." *Knight Ridder Tribune Business News,* October 23, p. 1

Office of Science and Technology Policy, Office of the President. 2006. "2006 Federal R&D Budget Facts." September 30. http://www.ostp.gov/html/budget06.html.

"Offshore Outsourcing Increasing from U.S." 2001. *ITworld.com.* http://www.itworld.com/Man/2701/ITW_2-28-01_outsourcing/ (accessed December 23, 2006).

"Opening the Doors: Governments Are Joining the Hunt for Talent." 2006. *Economist,* October 5. http://www.economist.com/.

Ostroff, F. 2006. "Change Management in Government." *Harvard Business Review* 36, no. 2 (May): 141–147.

O'Toole, J., and E. E. Lawler III. 2006. *The New American Workplace.* New York: Society for Human Resource Management.

Pascale, R. T., and A. G. Athos. 1981. *The Art of Japanese Management: Applications for American Executives.* New York: Simon & Schuster.

Peters, T., and R. Waterman. 1982. *In Search of Excellence.* New York: Harper & Row.

Pieper, R. 1990. *Human Resources Management: An International Comparison.* Berlin: Walter de Gruyter.

Pomeroy, A. 2005a. "Leaders Step Up Communication Efforts." *HR Magazine* 50, no. 11 (November): 14–15.

———. 2005b. "Leadership in Crisis." *HR Magazine* 50, no. 9 (September): 16.

———. 2005c. "Practice Makes Perfect for Leaders, Too." *HR Magazine* 50, no. 12 (December): 14.

———. 2006. "Rules Can't Ensure Ethical Behavior." *HR Magazine* 51, no. 11 (November): 14.

Prensky, M. 2004. "The Death of Command and Control? Leaders of Large Organizations in Business, Politics, and Even the Military Are in for Some Big Surprises." *Strategic News Service* Special Letter. http://www.stratnews.com/.

PricewaterhouseCoopers. 2007. "Was: Within Borders; Is: Across Borders; Will Be: Without Borders?" Tenth Annual Global CEO Survey. http://www.pwc.com/ceosurvey.

Rampat, A. 2005. *HR Transformation Survey: A Global Vision.* The Shared Services and Business Process Outsourcing Association (SBPOA) in Association with ADP.

Reddington, M., M. Williamson, and M. Withers. 2005. *Transforming HR: Creating Value Through People.* Westport, CT: Butterworth-Heinemann.

"Re-engineering HR Delivery at IBM." 2002. *Human Resource Management International Digest* 10, no. 6: 9–12.

Regnier, P. 2007. "Is It Time for a New Deal?" *Money* 36, no. 2 (February): 94–100. http://www.navy.mil/navydata/organization/org-shor.asp.

"The Revenge of the Bell Curve: As Talent Becomes More Valuable, Inequalities Are Rising." 2006. *Economist,* October 5, 1–3. http://www.economist.com/.

Reilly, P., and T. Williams. 2003. *How to Get Best Value from HR: The Shared Services Option.* London: Gower.

Rice, E. 2005. "2005 Trends in HR." Innovative Employee Solutions. http://www.innovativeemployeesolutions.com/knowledge/articles_04/04-article-13.html (accessed December 23, 2006).

Rivenbark, L. 2005. "Becoming a Strategic Leader." *HR Magazine* 50, no. 7 (July): 122.

Rodriguez, M. 2006. "HR's New Breed." *HR Magazine* 51, 1 (January): 66–72.

Rothwell, W. 1996. "A 21st Century Vision of Strategic Human Resource Management." Unpublished manuscript, report to the Society for Human Resource Management and CCH, Inc.

Rothwell, W., R. Prescott, and M. Taylor. 1998a. "Seizing the Future: A Survey of Trends Affecting the 21st Century." Unpublished manuscript, Pennsylvania State University.

——— 1998b. *The Strategic Human Resource Leader: How to Prepare Your Organization for the Six Key Trends Shaping the Future.* Mountain View, CA: Davies-Black Publishing.

Rowe, J. 2006. "Non-defining Leadership." *Kybernetes* 35, no. 10: 1528.

Saugatuck. (2005, May 19). "Outsourcing: Increasing Value." Downloaded on 23 December 2006 from www.saugatuck.com.

Society for Human Resource Management. 2006. *2006–2007 Workplace Forecast: Executive Summary.* Arlington, VA: Society for Human Resource Management.

Society for Industrial and Organizational Psychology. http://www.siop.org/tip/backissues/TIPApr02/05wentworth.aspx (accessed December 23).

"Strategic Change and HR Alignment at Reliant Energy." 2001. *Human Resource Management International Digest* 9, no. 6: 24–29.

Tai, B., and N. R. Lockwood. 2006. "OUTSOURCING: Outsourcing and Offshoring HR Series Part I." *SHRM Research,* Society for Human Resource Management, August. http://www.shrm.org/kc.

Toigo, J. 2001. "Storage Disaster: Will You Recover?" *Network Computing,* March 5. http://www.networkcomputing.com/1205/1205f1.html (accessed December 25, 2006).

Towers Perrin. 2005. *HR Outsourcing: New Realities, New Expectations; 2005 Study of HRO Effectiveness.* Towers Perrin, TP439–05. http://www.towersperrin.com/tp/getwebcachedoc?webc=HRS/USA/2005/200510/HRO_Report.pdf.

Toyota Motor Corporation. 2007. "Toyota's 50th Anniversary in America." News release, May 4. http://www.toyota.com/50th.

"Trends Propel New Human Resource Management Paradigm." 1996. *Human Resources Management,* p. 382.

U.S. Bureau of the Census. 2003. "Numbers of Americans With and Without Health Insurance Rise, Census Bureau Reports." Press release, September 3. http://www.census.gov/Press-Release/www/2003/cb03–154.html (accessed December 24, 2003).

U.S. Department of Commerce. 2006. "BEA New Methodology Shows R&D Spending Adds to GDP and Rate is Increasing." Press release, September 28. http://www.commerce.gov/.

U.S. Marine Corps. 1997. *Warfighting.* MCDP 1. Washington, D.C.: Department of the Navy, Headquarters, United States Marine Corps.

Urban Institute. 2006. *Work and Retirement: Facts and Figures.* Washington, D.C.: The Urban Institute. http://www.urban.org/publications/900985.html (accessed December 24, 2006).

Vashista, A. 2006–2007. "Trends in Services Globalization for 2007." White paper, Tholons. www.tholons.com/pdfs/trends-2007.pdf.

Vicere, A., and R. Prescott. Management Skills Assessment—HR. (1985–2007). The Pennsylvania State University, University Park, PA.

VisionPoint. n.d. *Generations: Harnessing the Potential of the Multigenerational Workforce.* http://www.visionpoint.com/uplds624/resources/10254_0f613i_generationsperspective012506.pdf.

"We Aren't Whining, We Do Work Too Much." 2001. *Seattle Post-Intelligencer,* September 1. http://seattlepi.nwsource.com/business/37360_work01.shtml (accessed December 24, 2006).

Wentworth, D. 2002. "The Schizophrenic Organization." Society for Industrial and Organizational Psychology. http://www.siop.org/tip/backissues/TIPApr02/05wentworth.aspx.

White House. 2005. "World Trade Week, 2005: A Proclamation by the President of the United States of America." News release, May 2. http://www.whitehouse.gov/.

White House. 2006. "Opening New Markets for America's Workers." Fact Sheet, September 30. http://www.whitehouse.gov/news/releases/2004/03/20040310-1.html.

"Why Do Organizations Outsource?" Software Engineering Institute, Carnegie Mellon University. http://www.sei.cmu.edu/sema/presentations/siviy/trading-places/tsld008.htm (accessed December 29, 2006).

Will, G. F. 2005. "What Ails GM." *Washington Post,* May 1, p. B7. http://www.washingtonpost.com/wp-dyn/content/article/2005/04/29/AR2005042901385.html.

"Work-Life Balance." 2000. HRM Guide. http://www.hrmguide.co.uk/general/worklife_balance.htm (accessed December 23, 2006).

"The World Is Our Oyster: The Talent War Has Gone Global—and So Have Talent Shortages." 2006. *Economist,* October 5, pp. 1–4. http://www.economist.com/.

Zwiljich, T. 2006. "U.S. Health Spending Nears $2 Trillion: Increases Slow but Continue to Tax Families, Economy." *WebMD,* January 10. http://www.webmd.com/content/Article/117/112504.htm (accessed December 21, 2006).

Index